PREPA**BAC**

Anglais

1ʳᵉˢ / TERMINALES toutes séries

Jeanie Maisonnave-Legendre
professeur au lycée David d'Angers, Angers
Michèle Malavieille
professeur au lycée Lakanal, Sceaux

CONCEPTION GRAPHIQUE : GRAPHISMES / MISE EN PAGE : ATELIER JMH / CONSTANCE CANAL

© HATIER PARIS JUILLET 1995 – ISSN 0295 7574 / ISBN 2-218-**71039**-0
Toute représentation, traduction, adaptation ou reproduction, même partielle, par tous procédés, en tous pays, faite sans autorisation préalable est illicite et exposerait le contrevenant à des poursuites judiciaires. Réf. : loi du 11 mars 1957, alinéas 2 et 3 de l'article 41.

Une représentation ou reproduction sans autorisation de l'éditeur ou du Centre Français d'Exploitation du droit de Copie (3, rue Hautefeuille, 75006 PARIS) constituerait une contrefaçon sanctionnée par les articles 425 et suivants du code pénal.

SOMMAIRE

COMPRÉHENSION

1. Comprendre un texte court **10**
2. De la compréhension au résumé **20**
3. Résumer **28**
4. Comprendre un texte long **34**
5. Traduction **47**

COMPÉTENCE LINGUISTIQUE

1. Le groupe nominal **66**
2. Le groupe verbal **70**
3. La phrase **84**

EXPRESSION

1. Méthode **92**
2. Fonctions de communication **102**
3. Rédaction **110**
4. Sujets de rédaction **118**

RELIRE SON DEVOIR **125**

DEVOIRS D'UNE HEURE

DEVOIR N°1 .... *134*
DEVOIR N°2 .... *135*
DEVOIR N°3 .... *136*
DEVOIR N°4 .... *138*
DEVOIR N°5 .... *139*
DEVOIR N°6 .... *141*

EXAMENS BLANCS

SUJET 1, SÉRIES L, ES, S (LV1) *144*
SUJET 2, SÉRIES L, ES, S (LV1) *148*
SUJET 3, SÉRIES TECHNOLOGIQUES (LV1) *152*
SUJET 4, SÉRIE L (LV2) *155*

CORRIGÉS *159*

MODE D'EMPLOI

Ce Prépabac propose un entraînement systématique aux **nouvelles épreuves du baccalauréat**. Il se conforme aux **instructions officielles** concernant les nouvelles modalités de l'épreuve.

Il propose des exercices développant **les compétences mises en jeu lors de l'examen**. Il se situe dans une perspective d'apprentissage et s'adresse donc aux **élèves de Premières et de Terminales**.

PLAN DE L'OUVRAGE

L'ouvrage suit les différentes parties de l'épreuve du bac : **Compréhension, Compétence linguistique, Expression**.

• **Compréhension**

Une série d'exercices entraîne à la **lecture sélective**, à la recherche des thèmes et des **idées clés**, au **résumé**. Huit textes littéraires ou journalistiques reproduisent les conditions de l'épreuve de compréhension à l'examen.

La traduction, qui est une partie nouvelle de l'épreuve, exige un entraînement spécifique. Des exercices ciblés (mot inconnu, contexte, registre de langue…) permettent d'en déjouer les pièges.

• **Compétence linguistique**

Ces exercices abordent tous les points de grammaire dont la maîtrise est indispensable le jour de l'examen. Ils mettent en jeu l'observation raisonnée de la langue.

• **Expression**

L'entraînement à l'expression couvre de manière systématique les points de **méthode** (faire un plan, une introduction, organiser ses idées, rédiger une lettre, un dialogue…), les fonctions de **communication** (mises en jeu en particulier pour exprimer son opinion, prendre position…) et les problèmes de **rédaction** (acquérir une expression correcte et diversifiée, utiliser les articulations logiques…).

• Les exercices de la rubrique **Relire son devoir** aident à une relecture efficace pour éliminer les erreurs rebelles.

• Six **Devoirs d'une heure** et quatre **Examens blancs** couvrant toutes les séries permettent de faire le point sur les capacités acquises.

QUELQUES CONSEILS

Pour l'élève

Ce livre vous entraîne à l'épreuve écrite. **Tous les exercices vous sont utiles, quelle que soit votre série.** Ils sont souvent accompagnés de conseils méthodologiques et d'aides.

Cependant l'organisation de l'ouvrage vous permet de travailler **selon vos disponibilités et selon vos difficultés.**

N'hésitez pas à vous servir d'un dictionnaire et d'une grammaire (sauf si l'énoncé de l'exercice vous demande de ne pas le faire!).

Notez et apprenez le **vocabulaire nouveau**, **les constructions que vous ne connaissez pas** et qui, réutilisées le jour de l'examen, vous feront gagner des points.

Pour le professeur

Vous trouverez dans ce nouveau Prépabac de nombreux textes littéraires et journalistiques **récents.**

Les **exercices corrigés** peuvent être donnés en travail autonome à la maison. Les **exercices non corrigés** vous aideront à évaluer vos élèves et les **épreuves complètes** à les préparer aux conditions **réelles** de l'examen.

SYMBOLES UTILISÉS

Le symbole **C** vous indique les exercices corrigés.
Le symbole ◆ vous signale les conseils méthodologiques.

PROGRAMME

Épreuves communes à l'ensemble des séries générales et technologiques
(B. O. du 28 juillet 1994)

RECOMMANDATIONS GÉNÉRALES
ÉPREUVES ÉCRITES

• **SÉRIES L, ES, S :** épreuve écrite de **LV1**, durée **3 h**, coefficient **4 (série L)**, coefficient **3 (séries ES et S)**
Cette épreuve a trois objectifs :
- évaluation de l'aptitude à la compréhension de la langue écrite,
- évaluation de l'aptitude à l'expression écrite,
- évaluation de la compétence linguistique.

L'appareil d'évaluation pourra porter sur un seul et même texte ou sur deux. Dans l'un et l'autre cas, la longueur totale n'excèdera pas soixante lignes (…). Les difficultés lexicales et contextuelles feront l'objet de notes qui les élucideront.

Par texte, on entendra soit un extrait d'œuvre littéraire (nouvelle, roman, pièce de théâtre, poème, essai, etc.), soit un extrait de la presse écrite (essai, éditorial, analyse de faits de société, etc.).

(…) Le support sera totalement ou partiellement commun aux trois séries. Les tâches à effectuer par les candidats pourront comporter une partie commune ou être totalement différentes en série L de ce qu'elles seront en séries ES et S.

- SÉRIE L

Dans cette série, l'épreuve pourra porter sur un seul texte ou sur deux. Lorsqu'elle comportera deux textes, ceux-ci pourront ou se compléter ou être mis en parallèle ou encore en opposition; le deuxième texte pourra également servir à l'exercice de traduction. L'étude du ou des textes pourra prendre la forme d'un commentaire guidé par des questions ou d'une discussion portant sur tout ou partie des textes.

Un travail sur la langue du ou des textes destiné à évaluer la compétence linguistique pourra s'intégrer ou s'ajouter à cette étude. Il pourra s'agir d'un travail sur le fonctionnement du texte (production du sens, organisation du discours, repérage des procédés rhétoriques, analyse de la valeur des formes grammaticales, etc.). Il pourra également s'agir d'exercices de reformulation, de transposition, de transformation, d'imitation, etc.

La traduction : le passage retenu pour la traduction en français n'excèdera pas dix lignes (…). Cette partie de l'épreuve aura pour but de permettre au candidat de montrer qu'il est apte à traduire en étant fidèle au sens et en respectant le niveau de langue.

- SÉRIES ES ET S

Dans ces séries, l'épreuve ne portera que sur un seul texte qui formera un tout cohérent. Ce texte unique pourra être soit le même qu'en série L, soit un passage du texte proposé en série L, soit l'un des deux textes proposés en série L. Les exercices destinés à évaluer la compréhension de la langue écrite porteront aussi bien sur le sens littéral du texte que sur sa signification profonde ou implicite.

Selon la langue, l'expression personnelle sera liée ou non au texte de support de la compréhension de l'écrit. Il pourra s'agir d'expression semi-guidée et / ou d'expression libre. Dans ce dernier cas, le candidat devra faire la preuve qu'il est capable de défendre un point de vue, d'exprimer un jugement, de commenter un fait de civilisation, etc.

Pour la compétence linguistique, on envisagera un large éventail d'exercices suffisamment diversifiés pour éviter un bachotage stérile. Il pourra s'agir d'exercices de reformulation, de transposition, de transformation, d'imitation, etc., liés ou non au texte.

La traduction : selon la langue, on pourra recourir à la traduction en français d'un passage du texte qui n'excèdera pas cinq lignes (…) et qui permettra au candidat de montrer qu'il est apte à traduire une langue simple.

• **SÉRIE L** : épreuve écrite de **LV2**, durée **3 h**, coefficient **4**

Cette épreuve a trois objectifs :
  - évaluation de l'aptitude à la compréhension de la langue écrite,
  - évaluation de l'aptitude à l'expression écrite,
  - évaluation de la compétence linguistique.

Le texte, support de l'appareil d'évaluation de la compréhension de l'écrit, sera soit un extrait d'oeuvre littéraire (nouvelle, roman, pièce de théâtre, poème, essai, etc.), soit un extrait de la presse écrite (éditorial, analyse d'événements ou de faits de société, etc.). (…)

Ce texte comportera de trente à cinquante lignes (…) et formera un tout cohérent. Les difficultés lexicales et contextuelles feront l'objet de notes qui les élucideront.

Les exercices destinés à évaluer la compréhension de la langue écrite porteront aussi bien sur le sens littéral du texte que sur sa signification profonde ou implicite.

L'expression personnelle sera, selon la langue, liée ou non au texte de support de la compréhension de l'écrit. Il pourra s'agir d'expression semi-guidée et / ou d'expression libre. Dans ce dernier cas, le candidat devra faire la preuve qu'il est capable de défendre un point de vue, d'exprimer un jugement, de commenter un fait de civilisation, etc.

Pour la compétence linguistique, on envisagera un large éventail d'exercices suffisamment diversifiés pour éviter un bachotage stérile. Il pourra s'agir d'exercices de reformulation, de transposition, de transformation, d'imitation, etc., liés ou non au texte.

La traduction : selon la langue, on pourra recourir à la traduction en français d'un passage du texte qui n'excèdera pas cinq lignes (…) et qui permettra au candidat de montrer qu'il est apte à traduire une langue simple en restant fidèle au texte.

• **SÉRIES SMS, STL** (toutes spécialités), **STI** (toutes spécialités) et **STT** (spécialité comptabilité et gestion, spécialité informatique et gestion) : épreuve écrite de **LV1**, durée **2 h**, coefficient **2**
L' épreuve a pour but d'apprécier le degré de compréhension d'un texte écrit et l'aptitude à l'expression écrite. Elle portera sur un texte d'environ trente lignes pris dans un journal, une revue, un roman, etc. (…)
La compréhension portera essentiellement sur le sens littéral du texte. Quant à l'expression personnelle , elle permettra au candidat de montrer sa capacité à répondre de façon personnelle à une ou deux questions simples portant sur le texte.

RECOMMANDATIONS SPÉCIFIQUES À L'ANGLAIS
ÉPREUVES ÉCRITES

• **SÉRIE L, LV1**
Étude du ou des textes.
Si la nature du texte ou des textes le permet, compréhension, expression et compétence linguistique seront associées. Pour entraîner progressivement les élèves à une approche méthodique des textes, on proposera des exercices qui permettent de repérer et d'analyser les procédés rhétoriques, les formes grammaticales, etc. Ces exercices pourront prendre la forme de reformulations, de prélèvements sur le texte, de réponses à des questions.
Seule la traduction fera l'objet d'une évaluation séparée.

• **SÉRIES ES et S, LV1, et L, LV2**
On pourra avoir recours aux exercices suivants : prélèvements sur le texte, reformulations, justifications, bref résumé, réponses courtes à des questions ouvertes. La traduction d'un passage pourra être demandée. Elle sera de l'ordre de cinq lignes.
Les exercices destinés à évaluer la compétence linguistique prendront appui sur le texte de support chaque fois que celui-ci le permettra.
Pour l'expression personnelle (de 300 à 350 mots), les candidats auront à choisir entre deux sujets dont l'un sera nécessairement lié au texte.

• **SÉRIES TECHNOLOGIQUES**
L'évaluation de la compréhension s'effectuera au moyen d'exercices qui ne mettront pas en jeu l'aptitude à l'expression. On pourra cependant demander des justifications par prélèvements sur le texte. Quant à l'expression écrite, elle prendra des formes diverses : bref commentaire du document à partir de questions ou bref développement sur un sujet proposé.

COMPRÉHENSION

1. COMPRENDRE UN TEXTE COURT 10
COMPRÉHENSION ÉCLAIR 10
MATCHING 11
RÉTABLIR LA PONCTUATION 12
TROUVER LE MOT MANQUANT 13
CHASSER L'INTRUS 15
INTÉGRER UNE INFORMATION 16
TROUVER DES ÉQUIVALENTS 18

2. DE LA COMPRÉHENSION AU RÉSUMÉ 20
FIND THE TOPIC 20
WHAT WERE THEY ASKED ? 21
CHOOSE THE HEADLINE 22
FIND THE RIGHT ORDER 23
TRUE OR FALSE ? 25

3. RÉSUMER 28
CONTRACT A PARAGRAPH 28
AFTER HEYSEL... 30
NO DEATH PENALTY FOR O J SIMPSON... 31

4. COMPRENDRE UN TEXTE LONG 34
IT IS ANNOUNCED FROM BUCKINGHAM PALACE... 34
MY LIFE AND TIMES 35
THE BOOK PEOPLE 36
MONDAY 38
THE DROP - OUT SOCIETY ? 39
THE LONESOME DEATH OF POOR HATTIE CARROLL 40
THE STEREOTYPE 42
THE SACRED CLOWNS 44

5. TRADUCTION 47
INFÉRER LE SENS 47
TENIR COMPTE DU CONTEXTE 49
DÉFINIR LE REGISTRE DE LANGUE 50
TRANSPOSER 52
MODULER 52
REPÉRER LES FAUX AMIS 53
TRADUIRE LES TEMPS 54
TRADUIRE LA MODALITÉ 56
TRADUIRE LE PASSIF 57
CHOISIR ENTRE PLUSIEURS TRADUCTIONS 58
TRADUIRE UN PARAGRAPHE 61

COMPRENDRE UN TEXTE COURT

■■■■■■ Compréhension éclair

Retrouvez le plus vite possible le contenu du livre, d'après les quelques lignes au dos de la couverture.

1. Is the man on page 40 painting his door ?
Is he trying to read a message scratched on the woodwork ?
Is he locked out ?
Is it really a door ?
The Mind's Eye will make you really think about pictures and want to talk about what you see. This is a unique collection of visual materials specially designed for use by language learners…

a detective novel - a book for nursery school pupils - an English language learning book

2. A … is an intermediate-level reference book for students of English as a foreign language. The new, third edition preserves the features that have already made the book so successful but the text has been thoroughly overhauled and now offers more guidance and fuller information.

a collection of American texts - the third edition of a grammar book - the new edition of a school book

3. *Manwatching* is a new, different way of looking at your fellow man. In *Manwatching* Desmond Morris has taken his work on human behaviour an important step beyond the controversial ideas set out in his earlier work, *The Naked Ape*, and presents the familiar in an unfamiliar light. He shows how people – even in a highly ordered modern society – signal to each other their attitudes, desires and innermost feelings…

a science fiction novel - a philosophy book - a study in psychology

4. …The texts are full. The vocal lines and arrangements for piano and guitar have been kept as close as it is possible to the way X… performs them. They have an aptness and basic simplicity which brings them within everyone's reach.

a book of folksongs - a book of poems - an opera libretto

5. An unforgettable story of the violent, intolerant, eccentric, humorous and prejudiced Deep South seen through the eyes of children.

an American play about racism - a collection of short stories about America and violence - a novel about racism in the Southern States

6. [...] a tour of England and Scotland in 1760, offering a striking panorama of the period, nevertheless a picaresque romance. The incidents of the journey are of the liveliest order with Matthew Bramble...

a collection of letters of 18th century travellers in Great Britain - a guide book of 1760 - a contemporary book about England and Scotland in 1760

Matching

C The following paragraphs summarize eight different contemporary novels. Can you match the summaries with the titles given below?

1. One, the son of a Boston millionnaire, the other a penniless Polish immigrant – two men born on the same day on opposite sides of the world, their paths destined to cross in the ruthless struggle to build a fortune. The marvellous story, spanning 60 years, of two powerful men linked by an all consuming hatred, brought together by fate to save and destroy... each other.

2. A spirited young girl runs away from the exclusive Kensington finishing school in which she has been placed by her cosmopolitan parents, and enters the School of Life. She is caught up in an extraordinary web of intricate and sometimes bizarre relationships dominated by the mysterious figure of Mischa Fox, an all-powerful, international tycoon from whom most of the major characters are trying to escape.

3. On the eve of an unusual voyage, a young woman reviews her life. Her story begins with a visit to friends in the country which, offering a contrast to the monotony of her home and family, serves as an awakening experience and an introduction to a new world. What follows is an enchanting and sensitive account of her struggle to retain the mood of her visit, and to achieve independent happiness.

4. With kindly humour, she relates all the difficulties and all the enjoyment of living in a small country community. M ... 's humour lasts even through staff problems, a village decision to marry her off and a nagging cleaning lady. But when she writes about her younger pupils, that amusement breaks into laughter.

5. Here we come up on my favourite of all the Millmoss discoveries, the Hippoterranovamus. One of Nature's most colossal errors the Hippoterranovamus ate only stork meat delivered in a land devoid of storks. Too large to become jumpy because of its predicament the novamus took out its frustration in timidity. A vast selection of ... in every kind of humour – animal, vegetal and mineral.

6. Ben Du Toit, a white South African, decides to investigate the death of a black friend in police custody after the Soweto riots. As he is drawn into closer contact with the brutal ruling forces of South African society, his curiosity becomes rebellion, and for an Afrikaaner rebel in white South Africa there is no way back.

7. Roger Quaife wouldn't have been seen dead on an Alderston march. His was a lonely ban-the-bomb-campaign waged from his seat in the cabinet and his office at the Ministry. His weapons were persuasiveness and a consummate skill in top-level diplomacy. And the stakes were far higher than a pair of blistered feet.

8. In this dramatic story X ... depicts, with sympathy and discernment, the complicated Oriental reaction to British rule and reveals the conflict of temperament and tradition involved in that relationship.

a. *The Beautiful Visit* (E. J. Howard)
b. *The Beast in me and other Animals* (J. Thurber)
c. *A Dry White Season* (A. Brink)
d. *The Flight from the Enchanter* (I. Murdoch)
e. *Village Diary* (Miss Read)
f. *Corridors of Power* (C. P. Snow)
g. *Kane and Abel* (J. Archer)
h. *A Passage to India* (E. M. Forster)

Rétablir la ponctuation

Dans les paragraphes suivants, la ponctuation a été effacée. Rétablissez-la.

◆ *Lisez attentivement le paragraphe et cherchez les repères logiques (accord du sujet avec son verbe, mots de liaison, relatifs, etc.).*

C 1. I won't get down thank you she said I just came to tell you that I'm going to be married what who to Cathy how grand when tomorrow said Cathleen quietly.

Margaret Mitchell, *Gone with the Wind.*

2. Next spring perhaps by next spring the war would be over and good times would be back and whether the Confederacy won or lost times would be better anything was better than the constant danger of raids from both armies when the war was over a plantation could earn an honest living oh if the war were over only then people could plant crops with some certainty of reaping them.
Margaret Mitchell, *Gone with the Wind*.

3. He has a great following Lai saw him you remember when she took Marjorie and Heather over to London I believe they saw him in *Macbeth* Marjorie read somewhere that only the greatest actors can manage the part of Macbeth the others don't have the voice for it.
Patrick White, *The Eye of the Storm*.

4. Sidney Radford after inheriting coal had sat about in an office looking important while somebody else managed the coal Gladys had money of her own was it from biscuits or those cakes and puddings full of burnt fruit and sand in tins anyway with their two fortunes [...] the Radfords could put on a show.
Patrick White, *The Eye of the Storm*.

5. A story is told about an organizer in another country adjudicating a case in the presence of a favorite disciple first he hears one side of the dispute reflects for a while and tells the plaintiff you're right the woman goes out and her enemy comes in the organizer listens gravely to her version of the grievance pauses and then says you're right the second plaintiff departs equally satisfied that a just verdict has been rendered as soon as the organizer and the young disciple are left alone the disciple breaks out but sir the two stories are completely contradictory and you told each one of them she was right that's wrong that's impossible you've made a mistake the organizer ponders for a moment and then says to the disciple you're right.
Susan Sontag, *Old Complaints*, in *I etcetera*.

Trouver le mot manquant

1 Dans ce paragraphe, un mot a été effacé. Retrouvez-le.

◆ *Cet exercice est destiné à développer votre faculté d'attention pour repérer les éléments significatifs d'un texte, l'inconnu à partir du connu. C'est bien entendu le contexte qui vous aidera à trouver ce mot.*

The ...... has created a mythology, iconography, and allegorical structure wherein America's past and present can be explored. André Bazin claimed that *Stagecoach* was an example of "classic maturity", and other critics have written of the "purity of the ......" as some people speak dangerously of the "purity of the race". But the ...... is, to quote Polonius, "tragedy, comedy, history, pastoral, pastoral-comical, historical-pastoral, tragical-historical, tragical-comical-historical-pastoral, and I might add, musical-comical-satirical-fantastical".

[...] ...... generally reinforced the theory that it's a man's world where men are men and women are... nowhere.

[...] The ...... is generally so unsmilingly in praise of the manly virtues that it has provided comedy with a theme against machismo and violence.

...... heroes are typically tall, laconic and drawling in tall stories such as *The Tall Men, Tall in the Saddle,* and *Tall Man Riding.*   *Films and Filming.*

2 Read the following paragraphs and try to guess the meaning of the word **tat** in each of them.

1. Over and over, the convention was described as "a rainbow of **tats**". No previous **tats** gathering could begin to match its diversity of age, income, race, occupation or opinion. There were 1,442 delegates. Three presidents' wives were guests... By the end of the Houston conference, the **tat's** movement had armed itself with a 25 point, revised National Plan of Action. By convincing majorities, the delegates called for passage of the Equal Rights Amendment, free choice on abortion, a national health insurance plan, custody for their children...   *Newsweek.*

2. I think **tats** are a threat. The big ones take people's jobs away, and the small ones are for lazy people – they do the work that people can do for themselves. [...] I don't like high technology coming into everyday work, because it means that work becomes mechanical and boring.

People don't have to use their heads or hands when they use **tats** ; they just aren't creative anymore. [...]

Anyone can use a **tat** – you just sit there and do what it tells you, you don't have to think or know anything. [...] These small **tats** are just gadgets, anyway, nobody really needs them. People buy them as a gimmick and play games on them – I think it's wrong to spend that much money on a toy. [...] The manufacturers who make **tats** talk about using them for education – I think that's terrible.   *Pace.*

3 These letters were published in a daily newspaper. Can you guess what they are about ?

1. My dog Daisy was pregnant and as I didn't like leaving her on her own, I asked a teenager to ....
While I was out, Daisy started giving birth prematurely. The teenager panicked, dialled 999 and shouted. "Daisy's having her babies". I arrived home the same time as the ambulance. I was most embarrassed but the crew thought it highly amusing.

2. I was ......ing for a friend when I thought I heard a sound upstairs. I went to investigate and tiptoed into a bedroom. The figure beneath the bedclothes seemed rather large for a three-year-old, so I threw back the covers – and came face to face with a startled 18-year-old.
My friend hadn't told me her elder son was in bed with flu !

3. We were very late home and I dashed in apologising to our new ......er. She had obviously had a difficult time with my two young rebels, because she said : "I don't blame you. I wouldn't hurry home either !"

4. As we waved goodbye to our young son and the ......er my husband emptied his hot, ash-filled pipe onto the gatepost. We returned home later to find people everywhere armed with buckets and a smouldering gatepost and fence. And in the middle of the lot was our ......er shaking from head to foot with shock !

A prize was offered for the best letter. Can you guess what instructions were given to the competitors ? Write the instructions in direct speech.

Chasser l'intrus

C Dans les phrases suivantes, certains mots ont été déformés. Retrouvez-les et rétablissez les mots qui conviennent.

◆ *N'utilisez pas de dictionnaire. Faites cet exercice en quinze minutes maximum.*

1. One of the main seasons that I left the US fourteen years ago to move to London was that I was thick to death of living in a word where there is total dependence on the automobile.

2. No manner how good you look, success in the pop word depends ultimately on the ability to make records that get through to pupils.

3. There are negative feelings about America which helped us to move – the materialism and the conformity, the lake of privacy and the superficiality.

4. Soap operas go back to the first radio cereals of the 1930s in the USA. In the 1950s they were transferred to television by large deterrent manufacturers who found they could read the housewise consumer by producing daytime serials around their soap commercials.

5. Usually, when a volcano erupts, people fly. In Hawaii, they flood by car, boat and helicopter to Hawaii National Park to view the fireworks.

6. In Manhattan, the towering buildings of Call Street block out a view of the sky, allowing a tunnel vision of one thing – the business of honey.

7. The American political horizon is chancing : minority Americans are seeing a "rainbow coalition" in the sky that may permanently change the political landscape. The "rainbow coalition" consists of Blacks, Hispanics, women, piece activists and environmentalists.

8. A famous lady needs your help. The Statue of Liberty is feeling apart, her structure is weakened : her petal is decayed. Even worse, Ellis Island itself has been deserted for decades and damaged by sandals. Please join our effort to cave the Statue and Ellis Island.

9. We are a nation of originals. Driven by the relief in ourselves and our ideals, fuelled by our independence of thought and action ; our probabilities are limited only by our dreams. We are Americans.

10. A Foof for anyone who doesn't know is a Fiend of Old Film, a fanatical collector of artefacts from past movies. One Foof may focus his or her love on the pictures of certain old-mime stars ; another may covet posters, period costumes or other relics.

Intégrer une information

◆ *Prenez bien connaissance de l'ensemble du texte avant de commencer.*

1 **Rewrite the following paragraphs adding all the information given below in disorder.**

1. In 1922 the mummified body of Tutankhamun was discovered in Egypt's Valley of the Kings. Its skeletal face was concealed beneath a funerary mask, an artist's likeness of the boy.
Today the name King Tut evokes the image of that mask, with its gleaming cheeks and limpid eyes. But a Miami orthopaedic surgeon wanted a more

scientific reedition of Tut's head. He commissioned two of the country's leading practitioners of face reconstruction Dr Clyde Snow and Betty Pat Gatliff, 52, a medical illustrator – both of Norman, Okla. *Life.*

Phrases to be included
- for $ 1,200
- who ascended the Egyptian throne at nine and died at 18
- , 55, a forensic anthropologist
- an amateur Egyptologist
- 3,274 years after his death
- magnificent, gold

2. February 5, 1983. A young bride appears on the walls of Paris. She promises to say "yes" in four days. "Yes" Our imagination runs wild for four days. In a fever of excitement we await the day. And finally, we have the answer : the bride says "yes" to the X department store collection.

This campaign is characteristic of an advertising technique called teasing. It involves catching our attention by arousing our curiosity. Teasing has been around for thirty years. It first appeared in France when a mysterious character called GARAP started popping up on walls before revealing his secret. GARAP was heralding International Advertising week by advising us to watch out : GARe A la Publicité. *B à T.*

Phrases to be included
- in 1953
- to what ?
- her eyes full of love
- when all will be revealed
- for advertising
- bridal
- week after week
- which is becoming more and more popular

2 Voici un texte et des phrases qui permettent de le compléter. Contractez ces phrases en un mot ou un groupe de mots, puis intégrez-les à la place qui convient.

The first comic books were simply bound collections of strips. They were for the most part crudely drawn but the format at least allowed for a whole story rather than a fragment, and the page layout could be more imaginative than in the strips. Then Superman appeared. His story, featured in the first full colour comic book had such an immediate success and appeal that it became the spearhead of a new medium. The new comics were essentially picture versions of the pulps, a form of escapist literature. These portrayed invulnerable heroes at a time when most people were at the mercy of events beyond their control, and the comics developed the theme.

Superman, appearing in the wake of the Great Depression, symbolised the triumph of the individual over the forces of evil.

P. R. Garriock, *Masters of Comic Book Art.*

- The first full colour comic book was Action and appeared in 1938.
- The Great Depression took place in America.
- The first comic books were strips taken from newspapers.
- Escapist literature was popular in the twenties and the years around 1930.
- The texts of the first comic books were very poorly written.
- Superman was enjoyed by lots of people from very different origins.

Trouver des équivalents

C Sous chacun de ces textes, vous sont donnés des équivalents de mots y figurant. Faites les substitutions qui conviennent.

◆ *Ces mots ne sont pas donnés dans l'ordre chronologique du texte. Prenez connaissance de l'ensemble puis faites les substitutions en pensant d'abord à la* **nature** *des mots.*

1. The things I used to dislike in America I now can't tolerate, such as the enormous materialism. TV crams everything down your throat. You feel a sense of deprivation if you don't have a jacuzzi. Over here, there's a great reluctance to have new things. When I got my telephone answering machine a few people in the village suggested that I was over the top and refused to leave messages. The paradox is that in the States you feel if you're not changing all the time something's wrong. When I go there I worry that my two-year-old son isn't going to be able to cope with the 21st century because he isn't into computers yet !

unwillingness - to manage successfully - to push - to feel underprivileged

2. Television has changed the way we view a catastrophe. Year by year, new disasters and their toll in death and destruction, human suffering and misery are brought vividly home to us. Few can have failed to be moved by images of starving children in sub-Sahara Africa or by the frantic efforts of rescue workers to dig out survivors from the rubble of buildings destroyed by earthquake in Mexico or to drag children from the clinging slime in Armero after the eruption of the Nevado del Ruiz volcano in Colombia.

The role of television and the newspapers should be neither underestimated nor denigrated – their attention is not, however, an unmixed blessing. Sadly, concern tends to become focused solely upon the immediate needs of stricken areas.

to pull out of - affected by a disaster - bits of broken stone - cost - to concentrate - something that brings comfort - thick mud - to die from hunger

3. In the past, all serious athletes needed was fine coaching, equipment, skills, training programs and desire. Now computers have added refinements that may change future approaches to any sport. Video games improve hand-to-eye coordination. Computer analysis of past competition can suggest strategy changes and highlight weaknesses. Specially made equipment, such as shoes, designed and manufactured electronically, can be better fitted.

to make better - abilities to do something well - to practice - to show clearly - to be the right size - to teach

4. The first time I told someone that their closest relative was soon to die, I felt the seductive thrill of power. It did not occur to me that actually it was an admission of impotence in the face of nature : nor that it was an outrage that a junior medical student like myself should be deputed to pass on this most delicate of messages on the grounds that everyone else was too busy to do it. I enjoyed for once being a person of the utmost significance.

reason - in fact - greatest - excitement - shocking fact - to come to one's mind

DE LA COMPRÉHENSION AU RÉSUMÉ

◆ Les exercices qui vont suivre ont pour but de vous entraîner au résumé. Ils illustrent les différentes étapes de la démarche type que nous vous proposons dans ce tableau.

Démarche	Objectif
Première approche du texte	Identifier le type de texte, son sens global, les renseignements fournis par la périphérie du texte.
Lecture analytique	Repérer les phrases-clés, les mots de liaison.
Élaboration du plan du texte	Distinguer les thèmes principaux des éléments secondaires (exemples, digressions, etc.).
Rédaction du résumé	Rester fidèle au sens du texte. Être concis : respecter le nombre de mots exigés.

Find the topic

Les titres suivants sont extraits d'articles de presse. Retrouvez pour chacun le thème de l'article.

◆ Trouvez le mot clé. Faites cet exercice le plus rapidement possible.

1. The Burger that conquered the country (headline).

2. As usual, Alice Cooper died on stage Wednesday night. The guillotine came slicing down, Alice's head dropped into a straw basket and a dense smoke screen covered the stage.

3. Haas said only the plane's captain should have the authority to ask for armed intervention, he's the best man on the spot to make that decision.

4. Ex-members of the group testified that the initial indoctrination included "very subtle brainwashing", emphasis on giving up school, family and friends.

5. The best way to prevent bad habits from becoming established is to encourage the development of good ones to replace them. It doesn't hurt to utilize a little common sense too : temptation is considerably easier to resist when it isn't present in the first place i.e. your shoes should be inaccessible. You can't expect too much of a young puppy !

6. Prune moderately by making a slanting cut above an outward facing bud.

7. Heat through, season, pour into bowls.

8. Now that women are climbing teasingly into slinky Thirties outfits, peering through eye veils or over outsize corsage, how are men going to face up – or rather dress up – to the challenge ?

9. Miss Whitfield was speechless after her shock success in the 200-meter breaststroke.

10. The programme has been offered to the whole TV network but other regions have not yet decided whether to take it.

What were they asked ?

Match the pairs speaking about the same topic. Underline the clues that guided your choice.

Derek Jameson
"Living without *Coronation Street* would be like being cast into perpetual darkness. I'm totally addicted to the box – it brings the entire world to my door – I'm obsessed with knowing what is happening."

Vivian Mitchell, secretary
"It certainly does. I've got three children, and all the hype makes them think they want much more than they need. It's stressful for parents. When it comes it's such a let-down. I don't know anyone who doesn't think ' Christ, is that it ? ' as they collapse in front of their turkey."

David Bell, naturalist
"My main concern is that there are one and a half billion women in the world of childbearing age. If they all got pregnant at one time, the world population would go up to one and a half billion – something very few people think about."

Tim Renton, MP
"Yes, I could provided my wife kept hers and there was also plenty of space for bikes on trains."

Donna Moore, student
"I'm more worried that a young man can be shot dead in the neighbourhood in cold blood than by anything happening abroad."

Mary White
"It would be a great relief. I could easily live without one, as long as I still had access to people, books and the beautiful countryside."

Jean Reiter, fancy dress hire
"People have no choice. They can't afford to spend like mad at the last minute, so they get things week by week. We start to get calls just before Hallowe'en. People ask for Santa Claus beards rather than for skeletons."

Dr Simon Valentine
"Life without wheels for a busy GP is unimaginable, impractical and impossible. I have been carless for two months since someone crashed into the side of mine. I've had to hire, borrow, take taxis and walk. It has been an absolute nightmare."

C   Question 1 : ... ? Who ? ...   Question 2 : ... ? Who ? ...
    Question 3 : ... ? Who ? ...   Question 4 : ... ? Who ? ...

Choose the headline

1   C Choose the most appropriate headlines. Justify your answers.

1. A total ban on smoking at youth hostels was rejected by the national council of the Youth Hostels Association at its annual meeting in Birmingham. But members' kitchens, dormitories, entrance halls, at least one common room per hostel, and rooms where meals are being served will continue to be smoke-free areas in the 253 YHA hostels in England and Wales.

Room for smokers
Total ban on smoking at youth hostels
Youth Hostels Association's annual meeting

2. Thousands of animal lovers marched in London to protest against the use of animals for scientific experiments.
Protesters gathered at the Earl's Court Exhibition Center to hear speakers. The demonstration was to draw attention to the 100 million animals said to die each year from scientific experiment.

Animal lovers' march
Vivisection protest
Death of 100 million animals

3. Britain's only full-time UFO investigator wants more research into what she claimed could be a "hidden invasion" by sophisticated aliens. Jenny Randles, of the British UFO Research Association, told a UFO experts' conference in Manchester that people who believed they had seen flying saucers could be having their minds probed from afar.

Space invaders
UFO experts' conference
Full time UFO investigator

2 C Find a suitable headline for this piece of news.

A man's ear, bitten off in a fight outside a Southampton pub, was being kept in a police station fridge as officers waited for the owner to appear and allow surgeons to sew it back on. Police, called to the *Captain's Corner* pub, found the ear on the ground.

3 Imagine the news in brief corresponding to the following headlines.

Detective accused of robbery
Madonna video banned
 C Famous paintings found in abandoned farm
Girl saved by baby brother
Man arrested after killing at hospital

Find the right order

1 Here are eight different tasks. Put them in a logical order using appropriate link words (for instance : first/then/afterwards/finally/after/before...).

1. Connect your ideas using joining words such as "on the other hand", "apart from that", "furthermore", etc.
2. Choose your topic quickly but carefully, i.e. one you can talk about at length.
3. Make sure your talk has : a beginning / a middle / an end.
4. If there is time, practise giving your talk from your notes in two minutes.

5. Go through your list and reject what is not relevant to your topic.
6. Decide if the topic requires a descriptive, personal or controversial approach.
7. Arrange your ideas into a logical order, using key words as headings.
8. Note down the ideas as they come to mind, as well as any vocabulary that relates to the topic.

Modern English International.

2 C Remettez dans un ordre logique les phrases suivantes de manière à constituer un paragraphe cohérent.

1. **a.** On the other was Bic's equally disposable model, famed for the slogan "Flick my Bic !".
   b. It was one of the hottest marketing battles in recent years. On one side was Gillette's inexpensive Cricket lighter, which could be used for months, then thrown away.
   c. "Gillette hasn't succeeded in the sale of Crickets for years," said Jeffrey Ashenberg, an analyst for the New York investment firm. "Obviously, it's decided. 'Enough'."
   d. But after more than a decade of struggling, Gillette last week conceded defeat. The Boston-based company said it planned to sell its Cricket line to Swedish Match, a leading European lighter maker.

2. **a.** When Charlie Chaplin died, Sir Laurence Olivier said of him : "He was, perhaps, the greatest actor of all time."
   b. Keaton, after all, knew a fair bit about comedy.
   c. Nevertheless, what he said about Chaplin merits serious consideration especially when taken in conjunction with Buster Keaton's assertion that Chaplin was "the greatest comedian that ever lived."
   d. Well, Olivier – himself regarded as the greatest by his contemporaries – is rather given to this kind of encomium.
   e. He also stated, posthumously, of Robert Donat that were it not for ill-health, "he would have had no peer throughout the world of acting."

3. **a.** Usually, Joan's depression lifts with the first sunny days of spring.
   b. She feels sluggish, irritable, uninterested in work or play ; she can barely drag herself out of bed. As a child, Joan's friends teasingly called her a bear, and her mother displayed a similar urge to "hibernate" each winter.
   c. By soaking up the morning rays Joan managed to shake her winter blues.
   d. Every year, as the days grow short, Joan K. senses the onset of a paralysing depression.

e. His prescription : get up early in the winter and go outdoors. The treatment worked.

f. Luckily, she phoned her psychiatrist who determined that her recent move to a dark basement apartment had prevented her seasonal cure.

g. One year, however, March came and went, and still Joan was depressed – to the point of suicide.

3 C Un certain nombre de phrases de ce récit ont été omises. Remettez-les à leur place logique.

While you two were at dinner I went to Valerie Hallstrom's place. It's an old brownstone with a basement and three floors. She owns it all and everything inside is very expensive. [...] I'll tell you in a moment what I found. Now that little inspection took me from about eight-thirty to nine-thirty. At nine-thirty the telephone rang. I sat in my car on the opposite side of the street and waited. At about ten-thirty a man, carrying a small briefcase, entered the house. He didn't come out. He didn't switch on any lights. I waited until I saw Valerie Hallstrom come home. I saw you pass by in the limousine. I saw the lights go on in the living room and in the bedroom, but I couldn't see inside because the drapes were drawn. He walked westward, across town. He flagged a taxi and beat the lights at the next intersection, so I lost him. I stopped at a pay phone and called Valerie Hallstrom's number. No one answered it.

Morris West, *Harlequin*.

He used a key.
I waited until it had stopped and left, by way of the basement.
I followed him.
About ten minutes later the man, still carrying the briefcase, came out.

True or false ?

1 Pour chacune des phrases suivantes, dites si elle expose une idée contenue dans le texte ou si elle le contredit.

C 1. Recognizing the importance of physical fitness is hardly a new idea. But the peculiarities of 20th century life has given the ancient adage a new meaning. Automation and high technology have removed physical exercise from countless daily routines. Many people feel a great need to give dramatic release to the accumulated stresses and pressures of office and home life. A sudden surge in the amount of people's leisure time has added to that need, particularly in countries where the workweek has been shortened because of the economic recession. *Newsweek*.

a. Never before has physical fitness been valued so much.
b. We no longer need to spend so much physical energy to accomplish our everyday tasks.
c. There's a lot of stress in our technological society.
d. 20th century workers enjoy more leisure time due to better conditions of work.

2. Although mass-tourism might seem to be an instrument for promoting peace and understanding among nations and friendship among people, its growth has been viewed in some circles with great concern. Many feel that exposure to hordes of visitors is bound to alter popular attitudes and beliefs, that tourism changes mentalities and spreads new concepts relating to work, money and human relationships, and destroys the ties that bind the people to their religions and ethics. In short, tourism is seen as a factor of acculturation in the worst sense of the term, and even of moral decay.
The Unesco Courrier.

a. It is generally considered that mass-tourism does little to improve the relationships between the various nations of the world.
b. This phenomenon can seriously affect the ways of life and the minds of people brutally subjected to values and behaviours totally alien to their traditions.

2 Voici des présentations de romans. Dans chacune, barrez les mots ou expressions qui n'appartiennent pas au résumé de l'histoire.

C • Maeve Binchy, *Light a Penny Candle*

Evacuated from blitz-battered London, genteel Elizabeth White is sent to stay with the boisterous Irish O'Connors. It is the beginning of an unshakeable bond between Elizabeth and Aisling O'Connor which will survive twenty turbulent years. Writing with warmth, wit and great compassion, Maeve Binchy tells a magnificent story of the lives and loves of two women, bound together in friendship.

• Mary Wesley, *The Camomile Lawn*

The Camomile Lawn moves from Cornwall to London and back again, over the years, telling the stories of the cousins, their family and their friends, united by shared losses and lovers, by family ties and the absurd conditions imposed by war as their paths cross and recross over the years.

Mary Wesley presents an extraordinary vivid and lively picture of wartime London : the rationing, imaginatively circumvented ; the fallen houses ; the parties ; the desperate humour of survival – all of it evoked with warmth, clarity and stunning wit. And through it all, the cousins and their friends try to hold on to the part of themselves that laughed and played dangerous games on that camomile lawn.

• Robert Silverberg, *Lord Valentine's Castle*

In an archaic, feudal empire, Valentine, an itinerant juggler, discovers through dreams and portents that he is his namesake Lord Valentine, his body and throne stolen by an usurper. He sets out to win his throne back. Valentine and his companions trek across the forests and plains of Zimroel to Alhanroel with its Labyrinth and then to the heights of power at Castle Mount. Silverberg's invention is prodigeous, a near encyclopedia of unnatural wonders and ecosystems. Silverberg, like a competent juggler, maintains his rhythm and his suspense to the end.

RÉSUMER

Contract a paragraph

1 Copy down the key sentences. Write a short summary of each paragraph. Give a title to the following paragraphs.

C 1. Most of the kids I grew up with left school at sixteen, and they'd be in insurance now, or working as car mechanics, or managers (radio and TV dept) in department stores. And I'd walked out of college without thinking twice about it, despite my father's admonitions. In the suburbs education wasn't considered a particular advantage, and certainly couldn't be seen as worthwhile in itself. Getting into business young was considered more important. But now I was among people who wrote books as naturally as we played football. What infuriated me – what made me loathe both them and myself – was their confidence and knowledge. The easy talk of art, theatre, architecture, travel ; the languages, the vocabulary, knowing the way round a whole culture – it was invaluable and irreplaceable capital.
Hanif Kureishi, The Buddha of Suburbia.

2. Consider the handicaps we have built into our system :
• The U.S. spends almost 12 percent of the gross national product on health care – far more than any of our international competitors. U.S. automakers, for example, spend as much as eight times more on employee health benefits than their Japanese counterparts. The irony is that we are far from being the healthiest people on the earth.
• We are the most violent, crime-ridden society in the industrialized world. None of our competitors suffers as much crime-related loss or spends as much to guard against crime as American industry must.
• The U.S. is the world's most litigious society. Two thirds of the lawyers on this planet ply their trade here. No other society spends as much time in court or as much money defending and insuring itself against lawsuits.
• No modern, industrialized society has the rate of drug-addiction, teen-age pregnancy and functional illiteracy that we do.
Taken together, these problems contribute as much to the decline of competitiveness as do ageing factories and crumbling infrastructure.
U. S. News and World Report, April 25, 1988.

3. He, for example, was a pure Italian, of peasant stock that went back deeply into the generations. Yet he, now that he had citizenship papers, never regarded himself as an Italian. No, he was an American : sometimes sentiment buzzed in his head and he liked to yell his pride of heritage ; but for all sensible purposes he was an American and when Maria spoke to him of what "the American women" were doing and wearing, when she mentioned the activity of a neighbour, "that American woman down the street", it infuriated him. For he was highly sensitive to the distinction of class and race, to the suffering it entailed and he was bitterly against it.

John Fante, Wait until Spring, Bandini.

2 C Contract this summary to 70 words.

Nancy Cato, *The Heart of a Continent*

Set against the unforgiving landscape of the outback, *The Heart of a Continent* tells the story of two generations of women and a dream that came true in the Australian skies.

Newly qualified as a nurse, Alix Macfarlane turns her back on her wealthy Adelaide home and family and sets out for the wild and dangerous great red centre of the continent in the first years of the century.

She meets and marries Jim Manning, a Queensland cattleman, defying him to build a clinic for the Aborigines. When he, in spite of her pleading, enlists in the First World War and is killed in Palestine, Alix is left alone, with only her baby daughter Caro and her dream. A dream that will become reality a generation later as the flying doctor service brings healing from the skies...

3 Contract this summary to 40 words.

George Orwell, *Animal Farm*

Mr Jones of Manor Farm is a lazy and thoughtless farmer, who is kicked off his farm by his animals. They rename the farm and begin to live by the principles of Animalism – "All animals are equal". As time goes by, the pigs obtain more privileges than the other animals, who find themselves in a worse position than previously when Jones was their master. In the final scene, the animals are unable to distinguish between the pigs and the humans who are visiting the farm.

Write your own account of a book in 50 words.

After Heysel...

After Heysel, European political leaders and sports officials swore it could never happen again. Now it has, with more than double the number of deaths that occurred in Brussels. And the violence, the haphazard killing, the desecration of a vivid and exhilarating sport is likely to recur, no matter what safety measures are taken to prevent it. Soccer has simply outgrown the limits of a normal sport. It has become the setting for a tribal warfare on a vast scale. It has generated true "fanatics" in such numbers that few European stadiums can accommodate the crowds that turn out for major matches.

Already, ordinary soccer spectators are guarded and constrained like convicts in a prison yard. Last year English police locked about 200 Dutch supporters in a special train to send them back home for fear they would meet and battle with their English counterparts. Everyone deplores the atrocities when they occur, yet no one wants to take the measures necessary to prevent them. A spokesman for FIFA, the international football federation, described the Sheffield Tragedy as "an English problem". Despite the horror, the game had to go on.

Commercial value : within the last two decades soccer has become a megabusiness. The walls of European stadiums are placarded with advertisements, many of them for the benefit of TV cameras back home. The commercial value of the sport is so enormous that no one involved can afford to interrupt the flow of receipts.

As the sport has been commercialized, the fans have become bestial. Soccer hooliganism was once regarded as primarily a British phenomenon. Now it has spread to the Netherlands, Italy, West Germany, and, to a lesser degree, France. But the swastika-bearing skinheads and fulltime agitators are not the only ones who perpetuate soccer violence. From the looks of them, the 3,000 Liverpool fans who forced their way into the Sheffield stadium last Saturday were conventionally dressed working-class young men from Yorkshire. They were not bent on troublemaking, but their outrage at not finding tickets to the sold-out match converted them into an ugly, and literally murderous mob.

Europe's wave of soccer violence is an illness of the psyche. Unemployed young men and others who are simply dissatisfied with their lot seek a spurious sense of identity in the packs of uncontrollable supporters. The sense of community that was once provided by schools and churches and nation-states has been replaced by the heady uproar of the crowd on a Saturday afternoon at the stadium. So long as soccer remains both big business and the stage for primitive tribal warfare, the chances are that the killing will go on. In the wake of the Sheffield tragedy, it is surely time to rethink soccer's place in European society. One way to start might be to take the game off Europe's television screens.

Newsweek, April 24, 1989.

1. C For each paragraph pick out the sentence(s) best illustrating the idea of the passage.

2. With the help of these sentences write a summary of the article (70 words).

3. C Find another title for this article.

No death penalty for O J Simpson

"Wise" ruling provokes calls of "double standards"

From David Usborne
in Washington

OJ Simpson was not about to "lose any sleep", according to his lawyers, over the decision late on Friday by Los Angeles prosecutors not to seek the death penalty in the double murder case against him. But in the streets and over the airwaves, an explosion of conflicting reactions has occurred.

Black leaders, who have lobbied the district attorney's office for weeks not to seek the death penalty against the former football star, expressed relief. But others, including feminist leaders, suggested that a double standard was at work : a famous figure was receiving special treatment.

Whatever the decision, controversy was inevitable. Mr Simpson, 47, is charged with the killing in June of his former wife, Nicole Brown Simpson, 35, and aspiring model Ronald Goldman, 25. Under Californian law, multiple murder is a "special circumstance" in which the death penalty can be sought.

After weeks of delay, which only added fuel to debate, a special panel of the office of District Attorney Gil Carcetti, said that it would seek imprisonment without parole, but not execution.

The decision will take some of the drama out of the case, which is due to begin with jury selection on 26 September. And it will deprive America of what surely would have been an unprecedented debate about the death penalty itself and its appropriateness as a deterrent to crime. Never before would someone so well-known have faced the gas chamber.

The move came as no surprise to most legal experts, who had been predicting that the death penalty would not be sought. In particular, it would have made it more difficult for the prosecution to obtain a first-degree-murder guilty verdict from a jury.

The decision was "very wise, very smart", said LA civil rights attorney, Leo Terrell. "It was legally correct, and definitely politically correct."

What particularly prompts accusations of double standards is the case of the brothers Erik and Lyle Menendez, charged with murdering their parents, and for whom Mr Garcetti is seeking the death penalty. Their defence claimed that they were victims of repeated parental abuse.

"What kind of moral or legal decision would merit the death penalty for 18- to 20-year-olds who killed their abusers, but not for a wealthy, independent adult who, they believe, killed the person he was abusing ?" asked Leslie Abramson, the attorney for Erik Menendez. "The only answer is that if you are a celebrity... you are going to be given considerations and privileges the average citizen does not get."

But John Mack, head of the Los Angeles chapter of the black Urban League, praised the decision, saying

"If you're a celebrity you are going to be given privileges the average citizen does not get"

O J : double murder charge

there were already too many blacks on Death Row. "We don't need another one there," he said. And it has been argued that, as a celebrity and role model for so many blacks, Mr Simpson is unlikely to receive a fair trial.

Meanwhile, rumours surface almost daily about the impending trial. Black comedian Bill Cosby was forced last week to deny reports that he was helping to finance Mr Simpson's defence, the cost of which is expected to run to millions.

The Independent, September 11, 1994.

1 Study the peripheral information provided by this article (do not read the article yet) : the titles and subtitles, the photo and its caption.
Then answer the following questions :
– What do you learn about O J Simpson ?
– What decision has been taken ?
– What reactions has it provoked ?
Summarize this information in one or two sentences maximum.

2 Now read the article carefully and fill in the following table, by ticking (✔) and quoting from the text.

Reactions to the decision concerning O J Simpson

Who ?	Approval	Disapproval	Arguments
...	...	...	...
...	...	...	...
...	...	...	...

– What is the opinion of the journalist ? In which paragraph is it expressed ?
– Summarize the article in no more than 70 words.

COMPRENDRE UN TEXTE LONG

It is announced from Buckingham Palace...

C Lisez attentivement le texte suivant. Quelle est sa nature (article de presse, extrait de roman, discours...) ?
Dans quelles circonstances a-t-il été publié ?

◆ *Vous allez déceler facilement les circonstances. Pour déterminer avec précision la nature de ce document, repérez le niveau de style ainsi que les éléments lexicaux qui peuvent vous indiquer le public auquel ce document s'adresse.*

"It is announced from Buckingham Palace that, with regret, the Prince and Princess of Wales have decided to separate. Their Royal Highnesses have no plans to divorce, and their constitutional positions are unaffected. This decision has been reached amicably, and they will both
5 continue to participate fully in the upbringing of their children. Their Royal Highnesses will continue to carry out full and separate programmes of public engagements, and will from time to time attend family occasions and national events together.
The Queen and the Duke of Edinburgh, though saddened, sympathise
10 with the difficulties that have led to this decision. Her Majesty and His Royal Highness particularly hope that intrusions into the privacy of the prince and princess may now cease. They believe a degree of privacy and understanding is essential if Their Royal Highnesses are to provide a happy and secure upbringing for their children, while continuing to
15 give a wholehearted commitment to their public duties.
I am sure that I speak for the whole House – and millions beyond it – in offering our support to both the Prince and Princess of Wales. I am also sure that the House will sympathise with the wish that they should both be afforded a degree of privacy.
20 The House will wish to know that the decision to separate has no constitutional implications. The succession to the throne is unaffected by it ; the children of the prince and princess retain their position in the line of succession, and there is no reason why the Princess of Wales should not be crowned Queen in due course.
25 The Prince of Wales's succession as Head of the Church of England is

also unaffected. Neither the prince nor the princess is supported by the Civil List.

I know that there will be great sadness at this news. But I know also that, as they continue with their royal duties and with bringing up their children, the prince and princess will have the full support, understanding, and affection of this House and of the country."

My Life and Times

I am a film addict and a book addict, too, but they are not equal in effect. The film satisfies something in me which books don't. The film satisfies the eye for one thing. I think, first of all, that one of the big differences between the two is that the film doesn't stay with you as a book does. A book is real meat and substance, and you live with it, and it nourishes you. A film, if it's a good one, is something which gives you wonderful moments and then fades away. Certainly you may recall certain things, but it doesn't hang on you for days on end, not even the best film, whereas a book you can't shake off. You live it over and over again for days and weeks, and it comes back to you again and again. It leaves a permanent impression upon you if it is a good book. Films don't do that to me. What I do notice about films is that certain characters become imbedded in the back of your head. You can bring them to life over and over again. With a book you never know how a certain character ever looked. You have to imagine him.

The motion-picture image is a very, very strong one. A poor film I can sometimes sit through, because something is going on ; indeed many things are going on at once. It isn't the story that holds me. There is color and movement. Action. There are also types I recognize, who are very close to me. You're observing living people, and they become more real, more close to you in some ways, than characters in a book. The characters in a book I never really visualize. They leave some sort of image, but it is blurred or vague.

Yet, you get something in books that no film can ever give : the associations which words conjure up, ideas that beg to be developed, and so on. These things can never be expressed in films. The film is too real, too concrete. What we love about books is elaboration, fantasy, complexity, for which the film has no time. The film has to be explicit. The film deals with tangibles.

Henry Miller, *My Life and Times.*

1 C In your opinion, which title suits this text best ?

In praise of literature
Books and films
The effects of the cinema
The age of the image

Justify your choice (50-60 words).

2 C In the following summary of the text, add the link words.

… films leave a visual and … transient impact in H. Miller's memory, books provide food for his imagination. … he remembers sequences from films, … these do not haunt him for a long time … films do not set his imagination going. Color, movement and action catch his attention. … he can even sit through a poor film. He identifies easily with the people on the screen who are so real, … the image of book characters always remains vague. This is the very reason … books leave him totally free to imagine. … words are less precise and more complex than pictures, books appeal to his mind's eye. … films appeal to his real eyes.

The Book People

"Would you like, some day, Montag, to read Plato's *Republic* ?"
"Of course !"
"*I* am Plato's *Republic*. Like to read Marcus Aurelius ? Mr Simmons is Marcus."
"How do you do ?" said Mr Simmons. "Hello," said Montag.
"I want you to meet Jonathan Swift, the author of that evil political book, *Gulliver's Travels*, and this one is Schopenhauer, and this one is Einstein, and this one here at my elbow is Mr Albert Schweitzer, a very kind philosopher indeed. Here we all are, Montag…
"It can't be," said Montag.
"It *is*," replied Granger, smiling. "We're book-burners, too. We read the books and burnt them, afraid they'd be found. Micro-filming didn't pay off ; we were always travelling, we didn't want to bury the films and come back later. Always the chance of discovery. Better to keep it in the old heads, where no one can see it or suspect it. We are all bits and pieces of history and literature and international law… All we want to do is keep the knowledge we think we will need, intact and safe. We're not out to incite or anger anyone yet. For if we are destroyed, the knowledge is dead, perhaps for good. We are model citizens, in

our special way ; we walk the old tracks, we lie in the hills at night, and the city people let us be. We're stopped and searched occasionally, but there's nothing on our persons to incriminate us. The organization is flexible, very loose, and fragmentary. Some of us have plastic surgery on our faces and fingerprints. Right now we have a horrible job, we're waiting for the war to begin and, as quickly, end. It's not pleasant, but then we're not in control, we're the odd minority crying in the wilderness. When the war's over, perhaps we can be of some use in the world."
"Do you really think they'll listen then ?"
"If not, we'll just have to wait. We'll pass the books on to our children, by word of mouth, and let our children wait, in turn, on the other people. A lot will be lost that way, of course. But you can't *make* people listen. They have to come round in their own time, wondering what happened and why the world blew up under them. It can't last. [...]
"When the war's over, some day, some year, the books can be written again, the people will be called in, one by one, to recite what they know and we'll set it up in type until another Dark Age, when we might have to do the whole damn thing over again. But that's the wonderful thing about man ; he never gets discouraged or so disgusted that he gives up doing it all over again, because he knows very well it is important and *worth* the doing."

Ray Bradbury, *Fahrenheit 451*.

1 C What do the following pronouns refer to ?

it (line 10) : ... **it** (line 14) : ... **it** (line 26) : ... **they** (line 29) : ...

2 C Complete the following summary with your own words or with words taken from the text.

In the excerpt from *Fahrenheit 451*, Montag meets people who have learnt the works of ...... by heart. At first, he is ...... but Granger explains that they have found ...... the safest technique since they had to ...... so much. Their aim is to preserve ...... and they do not seek to ...... anyone. They are waiting for the ...... to begin and end quickly. Granger expresses his ...... that some day, even if they have to ...... to pass the knowledge on to their children, they will be .... He says it might last only until another ...... but he is confident that ...... in the end will prevail against the forces that could rob him of his humanity.

Monday

What we decided, doctor, was that it would be best to lay our problems before a really competent professional person. God knows, we've tried to do the best we could. But sometimes a person has to admit defeat. So we decided to talk to you. But we thought it would be better not to come together. If one of us could come on Monday, Wednesday, and Friday, and the other on Tuesday, Thursday, and Saturday, that way you could get both our points of view.
A few debts. Not many. We try to live within our means.
Of course we can afford it. We don't want to spare any expense. But, to tell the truth, we picked you because your fee was more reasonable than some others. And Dr Greenwich said you specialized in problems of this sort.
No, we're not doing anything right now. Just riding out the storm.
Certainly not. That's what we're here to find out from you.
How much background do you need to know ?
Yes, we've both had physical check-ups within the past year.
Both born in this country, good native stock. Why, did you think we were foreigners ? You're a foreigner, aren't you, doctor ? You don't mind questions like that, do you ?
At the beginning, you can imagine, we felt very sure of ourselves. With a good income, a house with no mortgage, membership in three –
Sometimes. Sure. Doesn't every couple ? But they blow over. Then we usually celebrate by seeing a movie. We used to take in the plays at the Forum too. But we don't have much time for that anymore.
Oh, we dote on him. After all, when you have an –
Pretty regularly. Once, twice a week. Thank God, there's nothing wrong with that side of things.
No, it was the group that suggested we consult you. We're not claiming all the credit for ourselves. But probably we would have thought of it anyway.
All right, sure. We do. But what's wrong with that ? We really get along very well, considering the difference in our educational background.
Perhaps our problem seems ridiculous to you.
No, no, we didn't mean it that way.
All right.
That door ?

Susan Sontag, *Baby* in *I, etcetera*.

1 What is the literary device used by the author in this passage ?

2 Justify this choice.

3 Can you guess what the missing questions are ? Write them out.

▰▰▰▰ The drop-out society ?

America has been in a panic about education for at least a decade – and is right to be worried. Talk to businessmen and they will complain that they have a choice between providing new recruits with remedial education or moving their back-room offices abroad. America's high-school drop-out rate is at least 14% compared with 9% in Germany and 6% in Japan. The school year is 180 days – 60 days fewer than in some other countries. Japanese children do five times as much homework per week as their American counterparts. Even when they are working, American children are seldom stretched. The lack of a core curriculum encourages a shopping-mall approach to education : pile up the soft options and leave the hard stuff on the shelves. The result is all too predictable. American children perform poorly in international academic tests.

The most dramatic problem is the collapse of inner-city education. Ghetto schools are churning out children whose lack of mental skills and surfeit of emotional problems would render them unemployable in the third world, let alone the first. Schools based in crime-ridden and drug-driven neighbourhoods inevitably have problems with discipline. Some have to install metal detectors to keep guns and knives out of the classroom. Dropout rates of 50% are not uncommon.

It would be perverse to blame education for this social pathology. Children do not start toting guns because they flunk Shakespeare. But a reorganisation of American schools might do something to encourage the less academic children. The most glaring structural problem with American education is that it does not know what to do with pupils who are not bound for college ; it has no vocational stream. In importing the German university system, in the late 19th and early 20th centuries, America made the disastrous mistake of forgetting to import the apprenticeship system as well. For apprenticeships smacked of class-stratification, and America was hypnotised by upward mobility.

The Economist, November 21, 1992.

1 Give three reasons why, according to the journalist, *American children perform poorly in international academic tests.*

2 Explain the following sentences in English.

• ... *they have a choice between providing new recruits with remedial education or moving their back-room offices abroad.* (l. 3 - 4).
• *Children do not start toting guns because they flunk Shakespeare.* (l. 20 - 21).
• *For apprenticeships smacked of class-stratification, and America was hypnotised by upward mobility.* (l. 27 - 28).

The Lonesome Death of Poor Hattie Carroll

The different stanzas of this song by Bob Dylan have been mixed up. Can you put them back in the right order ? Justify your decision.

1. Hattie Carroll was a maid in the kitchen
She was fifty-one years old and gave birth to ten children,
Who carried the dishes and took out the garbage
And never sat once at the head of the table,
And didn't even talk to the people at the table,
Who just cleaned up all the food from the table
And emptied the ashtrays on a whole other level
Got killed by a blow, lay slain by a cane,
That sailed through the air and came down through the room
Doomed and determined to destroy all the gentle
And she never done nothing to William Zanzinger.

2. William Zanzinger who at twenty-four years
Owns a tobacco farm of six hundred acres,
With rich wealthy parents who provide and protect him
In high office relation in the politics of Maryland ;
Reacted to his deed with a shrug of his shoulders,
And swear words and sneering and his tongue it was asnarling,
And in a matter of minutes on bail was out walking.

3. In the courtroom of honour the judge pounded his gavel
To show that all's equal and that the courts are on the level
And that the strings in the books ain't pulled and persuaded
And that even the nobles get properly handled
Once that the cops have chased after and caught them,
And that the ladder of law has no top and no bottom.
Stared at the person who killed for no reason,
Who just happened to be feeling that way without warning,
And he spoke through his cloak most deep and distinguished
And handed out strongly for penalty and repentance
William Zanzinger with a six-month sentence.

4. William Zanzinger killed poor Hattie Carroll
With a cane that he twirled round his diamond-ring finger
At a Baltimore hotel society gathering.
And the cops were called in and his weapon took from him
As they rode him in custody down to the station
And booked William Zanzinger for first-degree murder.

                                                      Bob Dylan.

1 C The right order is : ...
Is there only one logical order ? If not, can you justify Bob Dylan's choice (refer to answer, p. 165) ?

2 Give a title to each stanza.

3 Fill in the following grid with information from the text.

	Hattie Carroll	William Zanzinger
Age	...	...
Social background	...	...
Activity	...	...
Disposition toward the other	...	...
Fate	...	...

4 This is an extract from the Fourteenth Amendment (American Constitution).

Section 1. All persons born or naturalized in the United States and subject to the jurisdiction thereof, are citizens of the United States and of the State wherein they reside. No State shall make or enforce any law which shall abridge the privileges or immunities of citizens of the United States ; nor shall any State deprive any person of life, liberty or property, without the due process of the law ; nor deny to any person within its jurisdiction the equal protection of the law.

In the context of the song, what is the important sentence in this extract ? Underline it.
Find sentences in the text :
– trying to show that the law is equal for all,
– proving the contrary.

5 Some sentences in the text are grammatically incorrect or familiar. Find them.

6 Why was William Zanzinger only condemned to a six-month sentence ?

7 Study these lines in the same song sung in French by Hugues Aufray. Discuss the decisions made by the translator. Do you consider these decisions necessary and effective ?

Hattie Carrol était domestique de couleur.
Elle avait cinquante ans et dix enfants mineurs.

Elle vidait les ordures et apportait les plats.
Elle s'approchait des tables mais ne s'asseyait pas,
N'osait pas adresser la parole aux patrons...

8 Sum up the song in ten lines, five lines, one word.

1. The stereotype

The sun shines only to burnish her skin and gild her hair, the wind blows only to whip up the colour in her cheeks ; the sea strives to bathe her ; flowers die gladly so that her skin may luxuriate in their essence. She is the crown of creation, the masterpiece. The depths of the sea are ransacked for pearl and coral to deck her, the bowels of the earth are laid open that she might wear gold, sapphires, diamonds and rubies. Baby seals are battered with staves, unborn lambs ripped from their mothers' wombs, millions of moles, muskrats, squirrels, minks, ermines, foxes, beavers, chinchillas, ocelots, lynxes and other small and lovely creatures die untimely deaths that she might have furs. [...] Men risk their lives hunting leopards for her coats, and crocodiles for her handbags and shoes.
[...] The men of our civilization have stripped themselves of the fineries of earth so that they might work more freely to plunder the universe for treasures to deck my lady in. New raw materials, new processes, new machines are all brought into her service. My lady must therefore be the chief spender as well as the chief symbol of spending ability and monetary success. While her mate toils in his factory, she totters about the smartest streets and lushiest hotels with his fortune upon her back and bosom, fingers and wrists, continuing that essential expenditure in his house which is her frame and her setting, enjoying that silken idleness which is the necessary condition of maintaining her mate's prestige and her qualification to demonstrate it.
[...] Because she's the emblem of spending ability and the chief spender, she's also the most effective seller of this world's goods. Every survey ever held has shown that the image of an attractive woman is the most effective advertising gimmick. She may sit astride the mudguard of a new car, or step into it ablaze with jewels, she may lie at a man's feet stroking his new socks ; she may hold the petrol pump in a challenging pose or dance through woodland glades in slow motion in all the glory of a new shampoo ; whatever she does her image sells. The gynolatry of our civilization is written large upon its face, upon hoardings, cinema screens, television, newspapers, magazines, tins, packets, cartons, bottles all consecrated to the reigning deity, the female fetish.

Germaine Greer, *The Female Eunuch.*

1 Tick the right answer.

This passage is :
- ❏ in praise of the enormous sacrifices accepted by men to satisfy women,
- ❏ a harsh criticism of the image of women in advertising,
- ❏ a women's libber's denunciation of the role allotted to women in our society,
- ❏ a description of the life of rich and idle women.

2 Find the topic sentence of each paragraph.

3 What sentence would best illustrate the general idea of the text ? Justify your choice.

4 Find equivalents for the following words in the text.

work hard : ...   go slow : ...
husband : ...   inaction : ...
premature : ...   statistical enquiry : ...
pillage (two words) : ... ...   provocative : ...

5 "*The men of our civilization... plunder the universe for treasures*".
Find sentences in the text which convey the same idea.
What criticism do they illustrate ?

6 Complete the following diagram

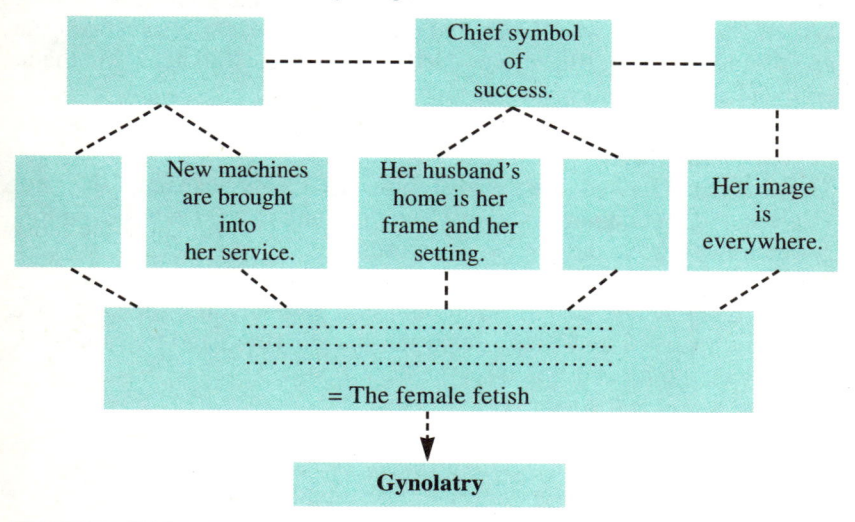

```
                          Chief symbol
        ┌─────────┐ ─ ─ ─    of      ─ ─ ─ ┌─────────┐
        │         │        success.        │         │
        └─────────┘                        └─────────┘
           ╱    ╲          ╱    ╲             ╱    ╲
     ┌─────────┐  ┌─────────┐  ┌─────────┐  ┌─────────┐
     │New machines│ │Her husband's│ │         │ │Her image│
     │are brought│ │home is her │ │         │ │   is   │
     │   into    │ │frame and her│ │         │ │everywhere.│
     │her service.│ │ setting.   │ │         │ │         │
     └─────────┘  └─────────┘  └─────────┘  └─────────┘
            ╲          │          ╱           ╱
              ..................................
              ..................................
                   = The female fetish
                           │
                           ▼
                      ┌─────────┐
                      │Gynolatry│
                      └─────────┘
```

7 What does the author mean by *gynolatry* ? (30 words)

8 Explain the title of the passage, of the book. (100 words)

9 Choose an ad in a magazine to illustrate the text. Describe the ad. Say in what way it illustrates the text.

10 Do you think the writer is rather objective, or rather prejudiced ? (70 words)

The Sacred Clowns

Officer Jim Chee belongs to the Navajo Tribal Police. He's investigating a murder on the reservation.

She poured the coffee into two tin cups. The pot held only enough for a half-cup for Chee and Blizzard. None for her. She put it back on the shelf.

"I know the boy," she said. "My grandson's son. We called him Sheep
5 Chaser. But I haven't seen him this year. Not for a long time."

Chee sipped the coffee. It was strong and stale. Through the doorway into the other room he could see a form laying motionless under a blanket. "Does Sheep Chaser have any good friends around here ? Somebody he might be visiting ?"

10 "I don't think so," she said. "He goes to live with his mother's people. The Tano people. I don't know anything about him any more."

Which was exactly what Chee had expected to hear. He translated the gist of it to Blizzard. Blizzard nodded and grunted. "Tell her I said thank you very much for all the assistance," Blizzard said.

15 "We thank you," Chee said. He nodded toward the doorway. "Is someone in your family ill ?"

She turned and looked into the bedroom. "That's my husband," she said. "He's so old that he doesn't know who he is any more. He has even forgotten how to walk and how to say words."

20 "Is there anyone helping you ?" Chee said. "Taking care of things ?"

"There is the belagaana[1] from the mission at Thoreau," she said. "He comes in his truck and keeps our water barrels filled and twice a week he brings us food. But this week he hasn't come."

Chee felt sick. "Is his name Eric Dorsey ?"

25 Grey Woman Benally produced an ancient-sounding chuckle. "We call him our begadoche, our water sprinkler. Because he brings our water. And because he makes us laugh." The memory of the laughter pro-

duced a small toothless smile. He has this thing, like a duck, and he pretends to make it talk. But the smile went away and she drew her hands up to her chest, looking worried. "Except this week, he didn't come." [...]

"Do you think he will come next week ?" she said. "If he doesn't come next week I will have to use less water."

"I will send someone out here to fill your water barrels, Grandmother," Chee said.

"I will send somebody from the mission at Thoreau or somebody from the tribal office at Crownpoint. And when they come you must tell them that you need help."

"But the belagaana has helped us," she said, looking puzzled, "in many ways." She pointed into the room, at the rocking chair. It was beautifully made with simple lines and looked new. "He made that for us, at the school I think. He said that chair would be better for my back when I sit beside the bed. And with the duck he would make my husband laugh."

"Grandmother," Chee said, "I think the belagaana who helped you is dead."

She seemed not to hear him. "He brings us food and he fills our water barrels and he took my man in to see the belagaana doctors. And he helped us when my daughter had rugs to sell. He told us the man at the trading post was not paying enough. And he sold them for us and got a lot more money."

"Grandmother," Chee said. "Listen to me."

But she didn't want to listen. "The trader had been giving us fifty dollars but begadoche got three hundred dollars once, and once it was more than six hundred. And when I had to sell my necklace and my bracelets because we didn't have any money he told me the pawn place[2] in Gallup didn't give us enough, and he knew someone who would pay a lot more because they were old and he got them out of the pawn and the man he knew gave us a lot more money."

Chee held up his hand. "Grandmother. Listen. The belagaana won't come any more because he is dead. I will have to send someone else. Do you understand ?"

Grey Woman Benally understood. She must have understood all along because even while she was talking her cheeks were wet with tears.

Tony Hillerman, *The Sacred Clowns*.

---

1. Mot indien pour homme blanc.
2. Endroit où l'on met des objets en gage.

1 Pick out expressions showing Grey Woman Benally is very old and very poor.

2 *Chee felt sick* (l. 24). Can you explain why ?

3 What adjectives could you use to describe the dead man as he appears in Grey Woman Benally's words. Justify.

4 *... the man he knew gave us a lot more money,* Grey Woman Benally explains (l. 59). Who is this man in your opinion ?

5 Pick out expressions showing the old woman is afraid of learning the truth about the belagaana's failure to come.

6 Find a title for this extract.

5 TRADUCTION

Inférer le sens

◆ *Inférer le sens d'un mot, c'est déduire sa signification à partir d'indices fournis par le contexte.*

1 C Dans l'article suivant, certains mots ont été effacés. Donnez leur sens en français.

Fatty Foods Find Favor Again

Americans are giving up the war on their waists as they … extra rich ice cream and half-pound burgers.

A … of thick, caramel-brown "Cappuccino Commotion" ice cream … the side of Julee Epstein's sugar cone until she … it up with her tongue. At the Häagen-Dazs … in midtown Manhattan's A&S Plaza, the 27-year-old New Yorker was savoring a dose of one of the most fat-laden desserts ever invented.

She is not alone. After years of warnings about the dangers of excess weight and fatty foods, some Americans show signs of … into what many dietitians consider bad habits. Perhaps because of relaxed attitudes toward excess weight, … brought on by diets or the stress of economic uncertainty, these consumers seem determined to enjoy the richest products of an endlessly inventive food industry no matter what the consequences.

Voici le texte complet. Lisez-le et modifiez, si besoin est, votre traduction.

Fatty Foods Find Favor Again

Americans are giving up the war on their waists as they guzzle extra rich ice cream and half-pound burgers.

A dollop of thick, caramel-brown "Cappuccino Commotion" ice cream crawled down the side of Julee Epstein's sugar cone until she scooped it up with her tongue. At the Häagen-Dazs outlet in midtown Manhattan's A&S Plaza, the 27-year-old New Yorker was savoring a dose of one of the most fat-laden desserts ever invented.

She is not alone. After years of warnings about the dangers of excess weight and fatty foods, some Americans show signs of sliding back into what many dietitians consider bad habits. Perhaps because of relaxed attitudes toward excess weight, craving brought on by diets or the stress of economic uncertainty, these consumers seem determined to enjoy the richest products of an endlessly inventive food industry no matter what the consequences.

The Guardian Weekly, July 25, 1993.

2 C Traduisez les mots et expressions figurant en gras dans l'article en vous aidant des remarques qui les accompagnent.

Twinkle, twinkle, shooting stars

Their life is little longer than that of **a mayfly's**. At 15, a female gymnast competing at the Olympics is mature ; at 17 she is a veteran ; at 19 she is a marvel of longevity.

If only their day in the sun was joyous, a glorious spreading of wings, a moment of **bliss** before oblivion. But for them, gymnastics is not an episode in childhood, but a **treadmill**. However incredible are the tricks that they perform with their tiny bodies, the rigours of learning them are **harsh** and cold. The sweet coquettish smiles that appear to be so innocent and spontaneous – and which, in Olga Korbut, their originator, probably were – have become **compulsory and rehearsed**.

When the three medallists of the event which the girls themselves regard as the big one – the individual all-round competition – attended a press conference on Thursday evening, they could hardly raise a smile between them.

The champion, Tatiana Goutsou from the Ukraine, 4ft 9in and weighing five stones, could not have been more matter of fact in explaining how she had done it. "We just went on training and tried **to overcome** our mistakes," she said. "We trained and trained and trained and managed to excel and went on with our training and tried to win the medal."

Shannon Miller, the silver medallist from the United States, equally blonde and **elfin**, but even younger, shorter and lighter, could have been the champion's twin sister. She said her medal was just a matter of "doing my routines and training hard".

Then the children **were whisked away for their dope tests**. Oh, happy world.

The Sunday Times, August 2, 1992.

mayfly (*l. 1*)
Décomposez le mot : connaissez-vous une partie de celui-ci ? S'agit-il d'un animal dont la vie est longue ou courte ?
Traduction : ...

bliss (*l. 5*)
S'agit-il d'un moment heureux ou malheureux ?
Traduction : ...

treadmill (*l. 6*)
À quel mot s'oppose-t-il ?
Traduction : ...

harsh (*l. 7*)
La connotation de cet adjectif est-elle agréable ou désagréable ?
Traduction : ...

compulsory and rehearsed (*l. 10*)
Retrouvez à la ligne 8 les termes contraires.
Traduction : ...

to overcome (*l. 18*)
Décomposez le mot.
Traduction : ...

elfin (*l. 22*)
Reconnaissez-vous un mot français ?
Traduction : ...

were whisked away for their dope tests (*l. 25*)
Traduisez essentiellement les idées contenues dans **away** et **for**.
Traduction : ...

Tenir compte du contexte

C Trouvez pour le même mot une traduction différente selon le contexte.

1. Set

1. They **set** the police on him.
2. He's trying to **set** my sister against me.
3. This piece of news **set** me thinking.
4. This has **set** everyone laughing.
5. That **sets** him apart from the others.
6. What time shall I **set** the alarm clock ?
7. This ring is **set** with diamonds.
8. Will you **set** the table for two, please ?
9. The second act of the play is **set** in the street.
10. The suitcases are ready, I think we're all **set**.

2. Man
1. He's a nice **man**.
2. The **man** is an idiot !
3. They fought to the last **man**.
4. He's his own **man** again.
5. **Man**, I was terrified !

3. Then, since, for
1. I'm coming back in two days, I'll call you **then**.
2. I think I'll have finished **by then**.
3. She lived in Paris, **then** she moved to London.
4. He kept thinking : "She never writes, **then** she has forgotten me."
5. **Then**, there is Mrs Smith. She must be invited to the party.

6. I didn't come **since** you did not call me.
7. He left home in 1970 and has not been heard of **since**.
8. How long is it **since** you last saw her ?

9. He's the right man **for** the job.
10. "E **for** Elizabeth".
11. **For** all that, you should have warned me.
12. She loved him, **for** all his faults.
13. They did not react **for** they had not heard.

▰▰▰ Définir le registre de langue

◆ *Il est indispensable, avant de traduire, de définir le registre de langue du texte (familier, soutenu, littéraire...). À la relecture, veillez à la **cohérence** de l'ensemble.*

C **Lisez les paragraphes suivants en anglais. Identifiez leur registre de langue. Surlignez dans la traduction proposée toutes les erreurs de registre et corrigez-les en conséquence.**

• Agatha Christie, *Tape-Measure Murder*

"Good afternoon, Miss Politt !"
The dressmaker answered, "Good afternoon, Miss Hartnell." Her voice was excessively thin and genteel in its accents. She had started life as a lady's maid. "Excuse me," she went on, "but do you happen to know if by any chance Mrs Spenlow isn't at home ?"

"Not the least idea," said Miss Hartnell. "It's rather awkward, you see. I was to fit on Mrs Spenlow's new dress this afternoon. Three-thirty, she said."
Miss Hartnell consulted her wrist watch. "It's a little past the half-hour now."
"Yes, I have knocked three times, but there doesn't seem to be any answer, so I was wondering if perhaps Mrs Spenlow might have gone out and forgotten. She doesn't forget appointments as a rule, and she wants the dress to wear the day after tomorrow."

« Bonjour, Mademoiselle Politt ! »
La couturière répondit : « Salut, Mademoiselle Hartnell. » Sa voix était extrêmement frêle et ses accents distingués.
À ses débuts, elle avait travaillé comme femme de chambre. « Je voudrais pas vous déranger, » continua-t-elle, « mais vous sauriez pas par hasard si Mme Spenlow est à la maison ? »
« J'en sais vraiment rien, » dit Mademoiselle Hartnell.
« C'est plutôt embêtant, tu vois. Je devais faire un essayage pour la nouvelle robe de Mme Spenlow cet après-midi. Elle avait dit à trois heures et demie. »
Mademoiselle Hartnell consulta sa montre. « Il est la demie et des poussières. »
« Oui, j'ai frappé trois fois, mais j'ai entendu personne bouger alors j'me suis demandé si Madame Spenlow était pas sortie, si elle avait pas oublié. D'habitude, elle oublie pas ses rendez-vous et en plus elle veut porter sa nouvelle robe après demain. »

- J. D. Salinger, *The Catcher in the Rye*

If you really want to hear about it, the first thing you'll probably want to know is where I was born, and what my lousy childhood was like, and how my parents were occupied and all before they had me, and all that David Copperfield kind of crap, but I don't feel like going into it. In the first place, that stuff bores me, and in the second place, my parents would have about two haemorrhages apiece if I told anything pretty personal about them. They're quite touchy about anything like that, especially my father. They're *nice* and all – I'm not saying that – but they're also touchy as hell. Besides, I'm not going to tell you my whole goddam autobiography or anything.

Si vous voulez réellement connaître mon histoire, la première chose que vous désirerez savoir est le lieu où je naquis, quelle fut ma triste enfance, quelles étaient les occupations de mes parents avant qu'ils ne me portent au monde, tout ce que l'on peut lire dans un roman de Dickens, en quelque sorte ; je n'ai pas envie d'évoquer tout cela. Tout d'abord, cela m'ennuie, d'autre part, mes parents auraient très certainement une attaque si je racontais quoi que ce soit de personnel les concernant. Ils sont fort susceptibles à cet égard, en particulier mon père. Ils sont absolument charmants, à n'en point douter, mais ils sont aussi extrêmement susceptibles. D'autre part, il n'est pas dans mes intentions de vous narrer toute ma pauvre existence par le menu.

Transposer

◆ *Traduire, ce n'est pas calquer une langue sur une autre. C'est souvent changer de catégorie grammaticale d'une langue à l'autre. Par exemple, un nom, une préposition devient un verbe, un adjectif devient un nom.*

C **Traduisez les phrases suivantes en transposant.**
Exemple : I said it **as a joke**. (nom → verbe). J'ai dit cela **pour plaisanter**.
1. They **kicked** the door **open**. (verbe → nom / participe passé → verbe)
2. You'll have to register before October **begins**. (verbe → nom)
3. He supervised the **whole** process. (adjectif → noms)
4. They ventured **out of doors** in spite of the storm. (adverbe → verbe)
5. They were **obviously** bored. (adverbe → proposition)
6. She **merely** nodded. (adverbe → verbe)
7. He was **rushed to** the hospital. (préposition → verbe / verbe → adverbe)
8. I've chosen the **wrong** book. (adjectif → adverbe)
9. **Just** answer my question. (adverbe → verbe)

Moduler

◆ *Effectuer une modulation, c'est changer de point de vue.*

C **Traduisez les phrases suivantes en vous aidant des amorces proposées.**
1. That's another pair of shoes. ...... *paire de* ....
2. Her cheeks were streaming with tears. *Son visage était* ...... *de larmes*.
3. I miss you. *Tu* ....
4. He took little notice of her. *Il ne* ....
5. She had a point here. *Sa remarque* ....
6. How long have you been waiting ? *Depuis* ....
7. He keeps complaining. *Il ne* ....

8. I've been ordered to take it easy. *On ...... de me ....*
9. He ran dry of ideas. *Il n'avait ....*
10. Let's leave this over till tomorrow. *...... à demain.*

Repérer les faux amis

◆ *Les faux amis sont des mots dont la forme est proche ou semblable d'une langue à l'autre mais dont le sens est tout à fait différent.*

1 Traduisez les phrases suivantes.

You look **terrific** with that green dress on !
You look **terrible** with that green dress on !

He was **attended** by a very nice girl.
He was **expected** by a very nice girl.

His father **blessed** him.
His father **hurt** him.

The police **controlled** the whole place.
The police **checked** the whole place.

He proved to be extremely **gallant**.
He proved to be extremely **courteous**.

Their **hosts** were delighted to see them.
Their **guests** were delighted to see them.

He was wearing a black **vest**.
He was wearing a black **jacket**.

He is the **virtual** leader of the party.
He is the **potential** leader of the party.

His words **unnerved** her a great deal.
His words **annoyed** her a great deal.

Patrons are sometimes hard to please.
Bosses are sometimes hard to please.

2 C Traduisez les phrases suivantes.

1. Could you **accommodate** four people for two nights ?
   Il **s'accommode** de tout.
2. Do you know the **actual** number of Indians living on reservations ?
   La Sécurité Sociale est un débat **actuel** aux États-Unis.

3. They had an **argument** over their daughter's marriage.
   Je comprends mal votre **argument**.
4. Glass is **disposed of** in special bins.
   Vous ne **disposerez** pas du dictionnaire.
5. A **dramatic** change took place after the elections.
   Il a eu un destin **dramatique**.
6. They **eventually** agreed to leave at six.
   Pouvez-vous **éventuellement** venir demain ?
7. Charles Dickens often **exposed** the evils of his time.
   Cette toile **est exposée** au Metropolitan Museum.
8. This is not a political **issue**.
   Un accord de paix a été signé **à l'issue** de la conférence.
9. Busing was organised to try and eradicate colour **prejudice**.
   Cet article lui a porté **préjudice**.
10. He **realized** too late it was a hazardous decision.
    Il a **réalisé** son rêve : devenir acteur.
11. Some 100 million Americans have **relatives** who arrived at Ellis Island as immigrants.
    Elle a de nombreuses **relations** à l'étranger.
12. He deeply **resented** having lost his job.
    Je **ressens** beaucoup de joie à l'idée de le revoir.
13. She was very **sympathetic** when my mother died.
    C'est un homme **sympathique**.
14. Soap operas are often quite **trivial**.
    Sa conduite est vraiment **triviale**.
15. The pioneers piled up their belongings in covered **wagons**.
    Certains trains américains ont plus de cent **wagons**.

■■■■■ Traduire les temps

◆ *Il n'existe aucune équivalence systématique entre les temps anglais et français.*

Soyez particulièrement vigilants pour ce qui est de l'emploi des temps du passé. Leur utilisation dépend souvent en français de l'aspect (par exemple : habituel → imparfait, ponctuel → passé composé, ou encore ponctuel plus littéraire → passé simple).

■ Traduisez les paragraphes suivants en prêtant une attention particulière à l'emploi des temps.

The lights were fading. A long beam shot across the darkness and ghostly words shone suddenly behind the curtains which parted with a rippling noise. Dreams were about to be made...
Stella Gibbons.

Les lumières .... L'obscurité ...... par un long faisceau lumineux et derrière les rideaux qui ...... en bruissant, des mots fantomatiques .... On .... (Place aux ....)

We have waited for more than 340 years for our constitutional and God-given rights. The nations of Asia and Africa are moving with jetlike speed toward gaining political independence but we still creep at horse-and-buggy pace towards gaining a cup of coffee at a lunch counter.
Martin Luther King Jr.

Cela fait plus de 340 ans que nous ...... les droits que la constitution et Dieu nous .... Les peuples d'Asie et d'Afrique ...... à la vitesse d'un avion à réaction vers la conquête de leur indépendance politique, alors que nous ...... à l'allure d'une voiture attelée afin d'obtenir que l'on nous serve une tasse de café dans un restaurant.

"Are you hurt ? " Pyle said.
"Something hit my leg. Nothing serious."
"Let's get on," Pyle urged me.
I could just see him because he seemed to be covered with fine white dust.
Graham Greene.

The Chens had been living in the UK for four years, which was long enough to have lost their place in the society from which they had emigrated but not long enough to feel comfortable in the new. They were no longer missed ; Lily had no living relatives anyway...
The Economist.

She wanted her life to be a movie magazine tragedy like the death of a young star with long lines of people weeping and a corpse more beautiful than a great painting, but she was never able to leave the small Oregon town that she was born and raised in and go to Hollywood.
Richard Brautigan.

Traduire la modalité

◆ *Repérez toujours la valeur exacte du modal.*
L'anglais est plus modalisé que le français : demandez-vous s'il est obligatoire de modaliser en français (par ex. : I can see... peut être rendu, selon le contexte, par "je vois...").
I can see him in the distance. Je le vois au loin.

◆ *Pensez à employer des adverbes, des tournures impersonnelles qui expriment la modalité en français.*
I must go now. Il faut que je parte.

◆ *Soyez enfin vigilant à l'emploi des temps. La marque du temps est portée par l'auxiliaire en français.*
You could have come ! Tu aurais pu venir !

C Traduisez les segments de phrases imprimés en gras.

1. All a long summer holiday I kept my secret, as I believed : I did not want anybody to know that **I could read... I suppose my mother must have discovered my secret**, for on the journey home I was presented for the train with another real book, a copy of Ballantyne's Coral Island. But **I would admit nothing**. All the long journey I stared at the one picture and never opened the book.
Graham Greene, The Lost Childhood.

2. About America : "**A brave, new world it might have become**, had we had the courage to turn our back on the old, to build afresh, to eradicate the poisons which had accumulated through centuries of bitter rivalry, jealousy and strife.
A new world is not made simply by trying to forget the old. A new world is made with a new spirit, with new values. **Our world may have begun that way**, but to-day it is caricatural. Our world is a world of things."
Henry Miller, The Air-Conditioned Nightmare.

3. Apart from the question of food, there is the question of energy. It seems clear that, if it were financially worthwhile, **fairly economical methods could be discovered** by which more use would be made than at present of energy from the sun.
And in theory there is no calculable limit to what can be got out of atomic energy. When people have discovered how to turn hydrogen into helium, sea-water will become their raw material, and it will be a long time before this source of supply is exhausted. Speaking of less specific possibilities, **we have to reflect that man has existed for about a million years**, and scientific technique for at most two hundred years. Seeing what it has

already accomplished, it would be very rash to place any limits upon **what it may accomplish in the future**. Scientific knowledge is an intoxicating draught, and **it may be one which the human race is unable to sustain. It may be that**, like the men who built the Tower of Babel in the hope of reaching up to heaven, so the men who pursue the secrets of the atom will be punished for their impiety. [...] **From some points of view such a destruction might not be wholly regrettable, but these points of view can hardly be ours.** Perhaps somewhere else, in some distant nebula, some unimportant star has an unimportant planet on which there are rational beings. Perhaps in another million years their instruments will tell them of our fate, and lead them to agree on an agenda for a conference of foreign ministers. If so, man will not have lived in vain.

Bertrand Russell, *The Limits of Human Power.*

Traduire le passif

◆ *Nombre de passifs anglais ne peuvent se rendre en français qu'en effectuant une transposition. On utilisera par exemple "on" ou une forme pronominale...*

C Traduisez les phrases suivantes en accordant une attention particulière aux formes passives.

1. Designer sales **are** usually **held** in London where most of the fashion agencies **are based**.

2. Leftovers **can be turned** into really exciting dishes – as these delicious recipes prove...

3. It **is said** that every day 1,500 more people arrive in Bombay to live, and, in Bombay, there isn't room for them. There is hardly room for the people already there.

4. I **was taught** how to walk around with a book on my head, how to pose in a bathing suit and how to frizz my hair... I don't mind **being looked at** in the street.

5. There was a time in China when female babies **were** routinely **abandoned** by families not wanting to feed unproductive mouths, but since the one-child-per-couple population policy began in the early 1980s, abandoning children has again become a problem that **is recognized** periodically in the Chinese media.

The Menincs **were not given** details about their adoptive daughter's background but learnt that she had lived at the orphanage for two years... The Menincs **were required** to submit reference letters, health certificates...
The Sunday Times.

6. The tearful face of a 6-year-old girl will save the lives of many people this Christmas in a drink-drive commercial which is so disturbing that television executives have banned it from **being screened** before 9 p.m. Tassita Haffendon stars in the 40-second advertisement which **will be shown** for the first time on Tuesday... It is the first of its kind to **be given** an adult rating.
The advertisement which **is expected** to provoke controversy among road safety campaigners portrays the ordeal of a girl whose father has killed another child in an accident caused by too much alcohol.
The Sunday Times.

7. What you have got to do is to destroy the thing that is upstairs – to destroy it so that not a vestige of it **will be left**. Nobody saw this person come into the house. Indeed, at the present moment, he **is supposed** to be in Paris. He **will not be missed** for months. When he **is missed**, there **must be** no trace of him **found** here. You, Alan, you must change him, and everything that belongs to him, into a handful of ashes that I may scatter in the air.
Oscar Wilde, *The Picture of Dorian Gray.*

Choisir entre plusieurs traductions

Choisissez la traduction exacte pour chacun des extraits suivants.

1. The new technique was aimed directly at the world's mass entertainees, and *its purpose was to manipulate their minds without their being aware of what was being done to them*. By means of specially designed tachitoscopes *words or images were to be flashed for a millisecond or less* upon the screens of television sets and motion picture theatres during (not before or after) the programme. "Drink Coca-Cola" or "Light up a Camel" would be superimposed upon the lovers' embrace, *the tears of the broken-hearted mother*, and the optic nerves of the viewers would record these secret messages, their subconscious minds would respond to them and *in due course they would consciously feel a craving for soda and tobacco*.
Aldous Huxley, *Brave New World Revisited.*

1. *its purpose... to them*
   a. son but était de manipuler leurs esprits sans être conscient de ce qui leur arrivait
   b. son but était de manipuler leurs esprits sans qu'ils soient conscients de ce qui leur arrivait
2. *words or images ... less*
   a. on projetterait des mots ou des images pendant une milliseconde au moins
   b. il était prévu que l'on projette des mots ou des images pendant une milliseconde ou moins
3. *the tears of the brokenhearted mother*
   a. les larmes de la mère au cœur brisé
   b. les larmes de la mère qui leur brisait le cœur
4. *in due course... tobacco*
   a. au bon moment, ils avaient besoin consciemment de boire un soda ou d'une cigarette
   b. le moment viendrait où, très consciemment, ils ressentiraient le besoin de boire un soda ou de fumer

2. *It is the very dead of winter : the trees black, the sky iron grey, the land the colour of a gun.* The drizzle comes in curtains from the West and the distant Brecon Beacons disappear with a drawing-to of rain. At the foot of the valley is a scene which takes the breath away.
George Catlin, the American artist who travelled with the first US dragoons in the 1830s painting what he saw, would have recognised it. So would the Blackfoot Red Indians. *For in this lonely, wet, cold yet achingly beautiful spot* in the back of a West Wales beyond, *stand thirty or so tepees*, sheltering from the freezing West wind.

1. *It is the very dead... gun*
   a. C'est le cœur de l'hiver : les arbres noirs, le ciel gris fer, la terre de la couleur d'un fusil
   b. C'est le cœur de l'hiver : les arbres sont noirs, le ciel gris fer, la terre a la couleur d'un canon de fusil
2. *George Catlin... recognised it*
   a. George Catlin, l'artiste américain qui voyageait avec les premiers dragons américains en 1830 en peignant ce qu'il vit, l'aurait reconnu
   b. George Catlin, le peintre américain qui, dans les années 1830, accompagnait les premiers dragons en relatant sur ses toiles ce qu'il voyait, aurait reconnu ce spectacle

3. *For in this lonely, wet, cold and yet achingly beautiful spot...*
   a. Car dans ce froid désolé et humide, cet endroit douloureux et beau...
   b. En effet, en cet endroit désert, humide et froid, et pourtant d'une poignante beauté...
4. *stand thirty or so tepees*
   a. se dressent trente tepees au moins
   b. se dressent une trentaine de tepees

3. *When the other kids asked what job my father did*, I said I hadn't got one because he'd been killed in the war – *which may have been true for all I cared*. But even at five or six, I thought my mother hadn't married because *no man would own me*, and I didn't much mind this, for I was used to it, and anyway I liked to have her for myself. Sometimes she bundled me off to Grandma's at Beeston while she went to Blackpool or London, but this was a glorious holiday because then I didn't have to go to school.
My grandfather was the best of men to me, though when he stayed home from work and drank a lot of beer he sometimes got nasty-tempered and called me a bastard – *which is what I understood a boy to be whose mother couldn't find a husband to live with her.*

1. *When the other... did*
   a. Lorsque les autres me demandaient le métier de mon père
   b. Lorsque les autres me demandèrent le métier de mon père
2. *which may have been true for all I cared*
   a. ce qui était vraisemblable pour ceux auxquels je prêtais attention
   b. c'était vraisemblable et d'ailleurs, ça ne me faisait pas grand-chose
3. *no man would own me*
   a. aucun homme ne voulait de moi
   b. aucun homme ne me possèderait
4. *which is what... with her*
   a. je pensais qu'il s'agissait d'un garçon dont la mère ne trouvait pas de mari pour vivre
   b. ce mot pour moi qualifiait un garçon dont la mère n'arrivait pas à trouver un mari pour partager sa vie

Traduire un paragraphe

1 Traduisez ce texte en vous aidant des indications proposées.

◆ *Style journalistique. Niveau de langue assez soutenu.*

The year was 1863, **and** Jules Verne decided to **take a break** from writing popular adventure tales to try his hand at **prophecy**.
He peered **into** the future and saw the streets of Paris **jammed with** automobiles. He also envisioned mass transit systems, the electric chair, even the fax machine. Yet his glimpse of the modern world was bleak and morose, **depicting** a society run by bureaucrats and philistines who **trample** classical culture in their frenzied pursuit of money, technology and power.
Verne's publisher, Pierre-Jules Hetzel, took **one** look at *Paris in the 20th Century* and advised the 35-year-old author to scrap it. "You took on an impossible task, and you did not pull it off. Nobody will ever believe your prophecies."
The Guardian Weekly, October 2, 1994.

• Valeur de **and** (l. 1) ? Pensez à changer la ponctuation si nécessaire.

• Attention au niveau de langue pour **take a break** (l. 1).

Pour **prophecy** (l. 2), opérez une modulation.

• Chassé-croisé : traduisez l'idée contenue dans **into** (l. 3).

• **Jammed with** (l. 3) ne doit pas poser de problèmes puisque vous connaissez **a traffic jam**.

• Le participe présent vous semble-t-il satisfaisant en français pour rendre **depicting** (l. 6) ? Pensez à sa portée.

• Pour **to trample** (l. 7), on peut certainement conserver la même image.

Valeur de **one** (l. 9) par rapport à **a** ?

2 Traduisez les paragraphes suivants.

1. He had been there for a long time. She could not remember when she had last looked across the lawn and he was not standing in the wide, well-clipped expanse between the buddleia[1] and the flowering quince[2], his shoulders sagging a little, his hands hanging limply at his side. He stood very still with his face lifted towards the house, as a tradesman waits who

1. Buddleia (lilas de chine).
2. Cognassier.

has rung the doorbell, received no answer, and hopes that someone will appear at last at an upper window. He did not seem in a hurry. Heavy bodies barged through the air, breaking the stillness with their angular cries. Currawongs[3]. Others hopped about on the grass, their tails switching from side to side. Black metronomes. He seemed unaware of them. Originally the shadow of the house had been at his feet, but it had drawn back before him as the morning advanced, and he stood now in a wide sunlit space casting his own shadow.

David Malouf, *The Empty Lunch-Tin.*

3. Small crowlike Australian birds.

2. A man's first instinct after a catastrophe as horrible as the earthquake that struck Kobe this week is to reflect on his impotence, and on the malignity of nature. If all the preparations of a tightly organised industrial society like Japan's come to naught, what hope for poorer and more chaotic places when nature strikes ? But this first instinct, though understandable, is wrong, especially if it encourages a fatalistic shrug of the shoulders. It is true that no engineer can design a building that remains standing when all the earth underneath it vanishes. And it is true that science cannot yet predict when and where earthquakes will strike, or how big an individual one will be. Yet in the case both of earthquakes and other disasters, people are better able than ever to know what dangers they face and, if not always to avert them, at least to soften the consequences. What is necessary is the will to act, the courage to learn, and – hardest of all – the ability to calculate the difference between preparedness and paranoia.

The Economist, January 21, 1995.

3. He felt troubled and asked : "Why don't you rise and go home, lady ?" She sputtered through her sob : "I have no home in this world !"
"Don't tell me ! Surely, you didn't grow up without a home all these years !" said the watchman.
"I lost my mother when I was five years old," she said.
"I thought so…" replied the watchman, and added, "and your father married again and you grew up under the care of your stepmother ?"
"Yes, yes, how do you know ?" she asked.
"I am sixty-five years old," he said and asked, "Did your stepmother trouble you ?"
"No, there you are wrong," the girl said. "She is very kind to me. She has been looking after me ever since my father died a few years ago. She has just a little money on hand left by my father, and she spends it on us."

The watchman looked at the stars, sighed for the dinner that he was missing. "It's very late, madam, go home."
"I tell you I've no home ," she retorted angrily.
"Your stepmother's house is all right from what you say. She is good to you."
"But why should I be a burden to her ? Who am I ?"
"You are her husband's daughter," the watchman said, and added, "That is enough claim."
"No, no. I won't live on anybody's charity."

R. K. Narayan, *Under the Banyan Tree.*

COMPÉTENCE LINGUISTIQUE

1. LE GROUPE NOMINAL
ARTICLES ET QUANTIFICATEURS **66**
FORMATION DU NOM ET DE L'ADJECTIF **67**
PRONOMS **68**

2. LE GROUPE VERBAL
INFINITIF ET FORME EN -ING **70**
FORMES INTERROGATIVES **71**
MODAUX **72**
PASSIF **75**
TEMPS **77**
"TIME" AND "TENSE" **80**
DISCOURS DIRECT / DISCOURS INDIRECT **82**

3. LA PHRASE
TAGS **84**
PLACE DE L'ADVERBE **84**
FORMES INTERROGATIVES **85**
PRÉPOSITIONS ET PARTICULES **85**
MULTIPLES POINTS DE GRAMMAIRE **86**

1 LE GROUPE NOMINAL

▰▰▰▰▰ Articles et quantificateurs

▰ Fill in the blanks with a(n) or the if necessary.

C 1. In ... New York City ... last week ... College Entrance Examination Board issued ... profile of ... 1,000,000 American high school seniors who took its Scholastic Aptitude Tests (SAT). ... profile revealed many noteworthy facts (... girls got ... higher average scores, for example, yet had ... less ambitious college plans than ... boys). But one seemingly ominous result attracted most attention : ... mean SAT scores had declined for ... tenth year in ... row.

2. ...purpose of ... advertising is to sell something at ... profit. It can create business for ... poor quality goods such as ... non-drip paints which drip at room temperature, or ... margarines which are supposed to spread smoothly on ... bread when straight from ... fridge, but which never do. ... right message has to be repeated in ... strict pattern and consequently it takes ... time for its effectiveness to be felt. What works in one case at one time does not necessarily work again in different circumstances. Yet ... advertising does work. It sells everything from frozen foods to ... political parties, building ... reputations which live and die according to ... season of ... year, ... current economy and ... fashionable whims of ... moment.

C 3. ... *Titanic row over ... new exhibition*
... National Maritime Museum sought to defuse criticism of its new exhibition of artefacts from ... wreck of ... Titanic by promising to convene an international conference ... next year to protect ... heritage of ships lost on the high seas.
... museum revealed its plans to stage a conference at a press preview of ... Titanic exhibition at Greenwich, south London.
Richard Ormond, ... museum's director, said ... conference would bring together representatives of seafaring nations, ... United Nations, salvors and academics to frame a new international protocol to protect historically-significant shipwrecks.
Mr Ormond said a new protocol was needed to prevent treasure hunters "looting the sea bed for their own gain". He added that wrecks could provide

historians with time capsules which would be lost if their contents were sold and dispersed. ... display of such objects has been condemned by ... several groups of nautical archaeologists who argue that ... Titanic was too recent a disaster to be significant.
But Millvina, aged 82, who was nine weeks old when ... ship sank and who also lost her father, said she had no qualms. "I think it's an excellent idea. It is part of our history."   *The Guardian Weekly,* October 9, 1994.

◆ *Il s'agit d'un article de presse. Dans le titre, les « règles » d'emploi ne sont pas les mêmes que dans un texte complet !*

Formation du nom et de l'adjectif

1 C -less or -ness ? Fill in the blanks with the appropriate suffix.
1. How thought ... and cruel of me !
2. The world was empty as they rolled without lights along life ... streets.
3. He stood there alone, in the dark ... of the night.
4. Waltzes always leave me breath ... .
5. I must have hurt his feelings. He wanted kind ... and I gave him none.

2 C Find the word which suits the context. Its origin is the same as that of the word between brackets.

1. Until the last few decades there was little public ... (*aware*) or concern about ... (*hazard*) waste.

2. Iris Murdoch's ... (*fiction*) world is one where life is irrational and often violent. Such a view of human nature may appear ... (*deep*) ... (*pessimism*) yet it is this concern with human morality and ... (*behave*) that makes her ... (*write*) so fascinating.

3. Our present civilization is a ... (*giant*) motor-car moving along a one-way road and at an ever-increasing speed. The only form of control the ... (*drive*) exercises consists in making the car go faster, though in his ... (*commit*) to achieving the highest possible speed, he has quite forgotten the purpose of his journey. This state of ... (*help*) submission to the ... (*economy*) and ... (*technology*) mechanism modern man has created is curiously disguised as progress, and the ... (*master*) of man over nature.

4. Many sophisticated Americans see beauty contests as ... (*sex*). The ... (*basis*) objection is that beauty contests legitimate the widespread ...

(*practise*) of judging and valuing women on the basis of their looks, instead of their character and ... (*able*).

5. Many people are waiting for the X ... (*crazy*) to pass. Others are ... (*conviction*) that the ... (*strong*) of their music and image will keep them at the top for a long time.

3 C First make compound adjectives using words from both lists in the appropriate form. Then fill in the gaps in the sentences below with these compound adjectives.

densely - ever - self - kind - business - wild - ever - well - age - well
to warm - to possess - old - eye - to populate - mind - to brighten - heart - to pay - to know

1. People sometimes need to have a heart to heart talk with someone, perhaps a close and ... friend to whom they can tell everything.
2. April is ... for its changeable weather.
3. "There's nothing new about it : it's the ... story of bad versus good."
4. He's ... for his work.
5. Business is booming for these ... Indians.
6. He became very strange and ... as if something were going to explode in him.
7. Whatever the cause, comets fall towards the ..., ... sun.
8. He works in Benwell Nature Park, in the centre of a ... poor area of Newcastle.
9. "My aunt will be down presently, Mr Nuttle," said a very ... young lady of fifteen.

Pronouns

1 Réunissez ces phrases au moyen d'un pronom relatif, en effectuant les changements nécessaires et en veillant à la ponctuation.

1. He is a professor. He has four children. Two of them were adopted.
2. The auction is expected to fetch £3,000 in total. It includes a large quantity of Victorian memorabilia.
3. He works for a firm. This firm makes "desktop" computers.

4. John Major launched an attack on Labour's plans for the regions. His own programme is severely criticized.

5. He will have to apologize for his conduct. He will consider it as a humiliation.

2 Fill in the blanks with reflexive, reciprocal pronouns or Ø.

1. To all these arguments she smiled, unwilling to commit ... before learning how she would like the town.

2. Who can resist the charm of one who discovers in others admirable qualities undreamed of even by ... .

3. The two boys were quarrelling ... .

4. You must forgive him today, he isn't ... .

5. The two girls hid their faces in ... 's necks and giggled.

6. The old women were sitting quietly on a bench, fanning ... .

7. She felt relieved : at least they hadn't shot ... .

8. They turned to ... to discuss the matter.

9. They went up to their room to dress ... for dinner.

10. Now you're beginning to think for ... instead of letting others think for you.

2 LE GROUPE VERBAL

Infinitif et forme en -ing

1 C Étudiez l'emploi des formes en -ing dans ces phrases et justifiez-les brièvement en français.

1. What you are really asking me is if it's worth saving.
2. I toyed with the idea of holding back the news but I couldn't do it.
3. He was sitting in an armchair dressed in silk pajamas.
4. He left his coffee untasted and began pacing the floor.
5. He stood there without speaking, and I knew he wanted to say something to me.
6. I couldn't help seeing that Mrs M. had her eyes on you all the time.
7. Seeing is believing.
8. Do you mind my smoking ?
9. I watched her crossing the street.
10. When are you coming back ?

2 Use the correct form of the verb given between brackets (choose between infinitive or -ing).

Boy : "For the past three days, I've been teaching kids how (*ski*). I've noticed that the girls seem very fearful of (*do*) something new. They hold back more than the boys do. If the kids have (*go*) down a steep trail, the boys don't seem (*mind*) as much as the girls."

Girl : "I think that the boys are just as scared but they keep it inside because that's what society tells them. Society says boys have (*be*) strong ; boys can't (*show*) their fears, boys can't (*cry*) if they're upset. I happen (*think*) it's beautiful if a boy cries. I really think it's nice."

3 Use the correct form of the verb given between brackets.

Bella Abzug, Congresswoman from New York City is famous for … (*wear*) hats. Once she explained : "I began … (*wear*) hats as a young lawyer because it helped me … (*establish*) my professional identity. Before that, whenever I was at a meeting someone would ask me … (*get*) coffee – they assumed I was a secretary. Nothing wrong with … (*be*) a secretary, but I had other plans."

... (*find*) a flat in London is very, very difficult. But London is also a very popular place ... (*live*) and each year more and more young people come to the capital ... (*seek*) work and independence.

A man was jailed for sixty days in Edinburgh for ... *(assault)* a policeman by ... *(throw)* a dog at him !

Formes interrogatives

1 C Find the questions corresponding to the following answer (there are several possibilities).

1. "It's red".
2. "A red one."
3. "The red one."
4. "Very hard indeed."
5. "Quite often."
6. "Three miles away."
7. "Windy and wet."
8. "Seven sharp."
9. "Twice a week."
10. "This one is the more expensive."

2 C Ask the question which corresponds to the group of words in italics.

1. John Dos Passos was born in *Chicago* in 1896. He went to *Harvard* University and graduated in 1916.
2. Based on the evidence of former years, *some seven to eight million Valentines* will be exchanged on February 14th.
3. In Great Britain, unemployment has been rising steadily *for 25 years*.
4. *Since the first performance in 1932* the theatre has held performances *every summer*.
5. Much of their leisure time seems to be spent *in watching television*.
6. "*No,* the pre-eminence of London as a financial centre is unchallenged."
7. Wimbledon, Barnes and Kew Gardens are *within easy distance* of where I live in East Sheen.
8. *As the surface of Venus is permanently hidden by a layer of cloud*, Earth-based observations did not tell us much.

9. *Orange juice* is more popular than grapefruit juice. For years, *Florida* supplied most of the orange juice consumed in the US. Now, with diminished supply and increased demand, *Brazil* fills the gap.

10. Giotto is a tiny probe, about the size of a car and costing roughly as much as a cross-Channel ferry, *about £35 million*.

3 Make up as many questions as you can corresponding to the underlined sentences.

This is what's true of me in brief. I'm female, age thirty-two, single, self-employed. <u>I went through the police academy when I was twenty, joining Santa Teresa Police Department on graduation. I don't even remember how I pictured the job before I took it on.</u> I must have had vague, idealistic notions of law and order, the good guys versus the bad, with occasional court appearances in which I'd be asked to testify as to which was which. In my view, the bad guys would all go to jail, thus making it safe for the rest of us to carry on. After a while, I realized how naïve I was. I was frustrated at the restrictions and frustrated because back then, <u>policewomen were viewed with a mixture of curiosity and scorn</u>. I didn't want to spend my days defending myself against "good-natured" insults, or having to prove how tough I was again and again. I wasn't getting paid enough to deal with all that grief, <u>so I got out</u>.

Sue Grafton, *"B" is for Burglar.*

Modaux

1 C Read the following sentences or paragraphs.
Are the modals used :
a. to express a degree of certainty,
b. to influence somebody / to offer / invite …,
c. to describe past or present ability / capacity ?

Tick the right box.

	a	b	c
Tired all the time ? You **can** beat it !			
According to the RAC, after you have phoned for help you **should** return to your car, lock all doors except the front passenger door and wait on the embankment until help arrives.			

	a	b	c

By law, a child **must** be suitably restrained in a car in a seat belt, with a booster seat if necessary, a child car seat or a carrier.

Earlier this year, the family arrived home one day to find water creeping up the garden towards the house. "We **couldn't** believe it," says Julia. "The river is normally several feet below the garden, but in the end it rose up into the house and the rooms downstairs were under a foot of water. The firemen **had to** carry the boys out through the windows. It was awful."

I **cannot** have slept long for when I woke the fire was still burning brightly. He descended the stairs, almost running ; it was not far now, now he **could** smell and feel it : the breathing and simple dark, and now he **could** manner himself to pause and wait, turning at the door, watching Miss Worsham as she followed him to the door ... Now he **could** hear the third voice, which **would** be that of Hamp's wife...

William Faulkner, *Go Down, Moses.*

"He **must** be a Southerner, judging by those trousers," suggested Harry mischievously.
"Why, Harry !"
Her surprised look **must** have irritated him.

F. Scott Fitzgerald, *The Ice Palace.*

Many's the night I used to sit here in this room and knit clothes for him when he was young. I even knitted trousers for him. And for all I know he **may** marry an English girl and where will I be ? He **might** go and work in England. He was staying in a house there at Christmas. He met a girl at a dance and he found out later that her father was a mayor. I'm sure she smokes and drinks. And he **might** not give me anything after all I've done for him. Iain Crichton Smith, *The Telegram.*

You **may** have seen my mother waltzing on ice skates in Rockefeller Center. She is seventy-eight years old now but very wiry, and she wears a red velvet costume with a short skirt... I don't know why I **should** find the fact that she waltzes so disconcerting, but I do. I avoid that neighbourhood whenever I **can** during the winter months, and I never lunch in the restaurants on the rink.

John Cheever, *The Angel of the Bridge*.

Nuclear waste **will** not disappear. **Should** governments try to hide it away, or keep it where they **can** see it all the time ? The world's nuclear industry **may** or **may** not last. The waste it has already produced in its first half-century **will**, however, be around for a very long time. Radio-active material produced today **will** still be dangerous in several million years, emitting particles that **can** cause living cells to mutate or die…

The Economist, December 3, 1994.

2 Examine the following extracts carefully, and identify the meanings of **would** in each case.

1. Garp investigated the city by day and found places to take Jenny to at night, and in the late afternoons when she was through with her writing, they would have a beer, or a glass of wine, and Garp would describe his whole day to her.
John Irving.

2. Jenny liked living with her son, in fact it didn't occur to her that they would ever live apart.
John Irving.

3. The coasting steamer passed the mouth of the river, dropped their mail, and went on its way. Guy busily wrote the letters which it would pick up on the return journey.
Somerset Maugham.

4. "Would you like me to come to the mouth of the river with you ? " "Oh, I think it would be better if we said goodbye here."
Somerset Maugham.

5. [He thought :] The huge white oxen would still be dragging their wains along the Tuscan roads, the cypress would still go up, straight as pillars, to the heaven ; but he would not be there to see them.
Aldous Huxley.

Write down the sentence(s) in which **would** implies :
– habit in the past,
– polite request,
– conditional,
– future in the past.

3 Identify the meanings of **would** in this paragraph, then translate the sentences in which they appear into French.

Ada had an immense capacity for fantasy when it came to swashbuckling adventures. She wanted to dress up as a man, complete with big hat and curling feather, and ride off into the night. If I would be a maiden in distress, or captured by highwaymen, she would rescue me. Sometimes she would tie me up with a skipping rope and leave me alone in the dark, so she could come down and free me from dragons, or enemy soldiers or whatever, and I would stand in the dark, listening, hearing voices far off or, worse still, hearing nothing but my own breathing, my own heart beating, while I waited for her to find me.
Eva Figes, *The Seven Ages*.

Passif

1 C Transposez les phrases suivantes en prenant le mot en italique comme sujet.
Le changement de sujet implique une transposition du verbe de la voix passive à la voix active ou l'inverse.

1. The power of the officials immediately impressed *them*.
2. Unless Europe is united, its voice will be ignored by *the world*.
3. Delighted crowds welcomed *the Queen and the Duke of Edinburgh*.
4. Next month I shall suggest how we might achieve *this*.
5. I only read detective fiction when I am interested in *the characters and the background*.
6. Human intelligence and ingenuity are going to solve *this problem*.
7. Do not trust *them*.
8. They were showing *him* the new offices.
9. Did they actually give *her* the new job ?
10. The production is being mounted by *Glyndebourne*.

2 Rewrite the following sentences in the passive, omitting the agent with by when not necessary.

1. Someone has invited him to the party.
2. The papers said he had been killed in an accident.
3. People say she is very strict.
4. The police arrested the three men a few days later.

5. England beat France in yesterday's rugby match.
6. Fire destroyed a whole forest in the south of France last summer.
7. They will equip all new models of this car with electric windows.
8. Someone has stolen one thousand pounds' worth of jewellery.
9. Someone told her to wait.
10. Her father gave her a birthday present. (*two solutions*)

3 C Fill in the blanks with the appropriate form of the verb or verbal group given between brackets : past tense (preterite), active or passive ?

In May a disturbing thing ... (*to happen*) in the chess world. At a tournament in Munich, a computer chess program powered by an intel Pentium chip ... (*to beat*) the world champion, Garry Kasparov. And it ... (*cannot explain*) away as a freak result. Pentium-Fritz 3 had already defeated several grandmasters. With technology advancing swiftly, there were gloomy predictions that this ... (*to mark*) the end of human dominance in the game.
Chess machines are not a modern phenomenon. The first, known as the Turk ... (*to invent*) in 1769 by Wolfgang von Kempelen to entertain Empress Maria Theresa of Austria, and perhaps take her mind off her 16 children. The Turk ... (*to defeat*) many notable figures, including Napoleon in 1809, before perishing by fire in 1854. There was, of course, enough room for a man to hide inside. [...]
The Munich event has to be seen in its context. In tournament chess, a game is played at a standard rate of 40 moves in two hours. The Munich game was "blitz chess", in which players have just five minutes for all their moves. When they ... (*to play*) against the computer they ... (*to give*) an extra minute, but this hardly ... (*to make up*) for the fact that they were playing on a computer screen with a mouse.
A grandmaster is accustomed to playing on a wooden board with adjacent clock and he can, if necessary, complete a whole game in less than a minute. Even so, against a computer the human is at a disadvantage. [...] In 1993 the machines ... (*to come*) ahead of the human players for the first time.

The Economist, July 30, 1994

4 C Read the following passage. Pick out the different passive forms. Justify their use.

Marvin Macy was one of seven unwanted children whose parents could hardly be called parents at all ; these parents were wild younguns who liked to fish and roam around the swamp. Their own children, and there was a new one almost every year, were only a nuisance to them. At night when they came home from the mill they would look at the children as though they did not know wherever they had come from. If the children cried they were beaten, and the first thing they learned in this world was to seek the darkest corner of the room and try to hide themselves as best they could. They were as thin as little white-haired ghosts, and they did not speak, not even to each other. Finally, they were abandoned by their parents altogether and left to the mercies of the town. It was a hard winter, with the mill closed down almost three months, and much misery everywhere. But this is not a town to let white orphans perish in the road before your eyes. So here is what came about : the eldest child, who was eight years old, walked into Cheehaw and disappeared – perhaps he took a freight train somewhere and went out into the world, nobody knows. Three other children were boarded out amongst the town, being sent around from one kitchen to another, and as they were delicate they died before Easter time. The last two children were Marvin Macy and Henry Macy, and they were taken into a home. There was a good woman in the town named Mrs Mary Hale, and she took Marvin Macy and Henry Macy and loved them as her own. They were raised in her household and treated well.

But the hearts of small children are delicate organs. A cruel beginning in this world can twist them into curious shapes. The heart of a hurt child can shrink so that forever afterward it is hard and pitted as the seed of a peach.

Carson Mc Cullers, The Ballad of the Sad Café.

Temps

1 C Justifiez en français l'utilisation des temps du passé dans les phrases suivantes.

1. "But I've never seen anyone saner," said Angela.
"He certainly has that air," said the doctor, "and in the last twenty years we have treated him as such…"   Evelyn Waugh.

2. "Perhaps you had better go to a doctor, ma'am." She replied that she had already seen a doctor.   Thomas Hardy.

3. "When I awoke I could not remember where I was," she added, "till the clock striking two reminded me."   Thomas Hardy.

4. And that night the dog was so tired that he didn't pace around the café. He slept on the floor as if he were sick.   John Irving.

5. I met him long ago, but I haven't seen him since.

2 C Put the verbs in brackets in the correct tense. Before deciding, analyse the situation in each sentence carefully.
1. You ... me, I ... a red coat. (*recognize, wear*)
2. "Why are you going to bed so early ?" "I ... at six tomorrow." (*get up*)
3. What ... with him ? He's drunk. (*we do*)
4. ... my cigarettes, please ? (*you bring*)
5. The sky is getting darker and darker, I think ... . (*rain*)
6. ... dinner now ? (*we have*)

3 C Complete the following passage with the verbs provided in the past.
It ... still early. I ... to go back to the hotel with its plastic starlets and greying agents. I ... to be anonymous, free to talk mundane things : the cost of beefsteak, the film on T.V. and how the girls ... what they used to be. I ... low life. It's simpler to live and there ... more friends to share it with you. I ... into a bar on the Strip, dim and almost deserted. I ... a bourbon, ... a beer for the house and ... down to half an hour of laconic lament with the barman.
We ... the Middle East and ... on the scandals of the Administration when the telephone ... .   Morris West, *Harlequin*.

be - not care - want - not be - like - be - pull - order - buy - settle - just sort out - start - ring

4 Fill in the blanks with the correct tenses of the verbs between brackets.
Today Britain ... (*move*) irreversibly closer to Europe. Lorries ... (*be carried*) on the shuttle service between Folkestone and Calais for the past six months, and freight trains from various parts of the UK ... (*roll*) through during the night. But the start of commercial train services from London to Paris and Brussels ... (*mark*) the real opening of the Channel tunnel. [...] The tunnel ... (*be*) a tremendous engineering achievement and a great visionary project – and there ... (*be*) few of those to celebrate in the past few decades.   *The Independent,* November 14, 1994.

5 Transposez les phrases et paragraphes suivants en situant le récit dans le passé.
◆ *Attention non seulement aux temps mais aux adverbes, démonstratifs...*

She says that her mother died five years ago.
When it gets dark, he'll draw the curtains.
They are telling her that their friends left yesterday.
He is telling you to do it tomorrow.
He is sure he will be here again in two days.
He explains that he has bought these books for her mother.

The sea winds are moving in to invest the upper town with their damp coolness but as yet one feels them spasmodically. L. Durrell.

Soon the mist will vanish and the light will blaze up on the cutlery and white cloth... L. Durrell.

The chief hinted yesterday that there are still harder things he will ask, and indeed the young demonstrator is dissatisfied that they have not been asked at once. A. Paton.

It is some while since the pain has returned, now that I am lying still and holding my breath ; that seems to me just as important. G. Greene.

The sea begins to draw away from the Cinque Port, leaving it high and dry with a stretch of sea... E. Bowen *(start with : Centuries ago...).*

My mind is laughing at little Jimson when he holds my hand and tells me he can make me so rich and give me furs and jewels. J. Cary.

When the curtain falls abruptly closed and the window is again empty, Joel, reawakening, takes a backward step and stumbles against the bell : one raucous, cracked note rings out shattering the hot stillness. T. Capote.

6 C Read the following excerpt and complete with the verbs provided in the past. Make the necessary adjustments.

When Lucy was twenty-nine her mother ... . Technically, she ..., having completed some years before the laborious process of divorcing an absent husband, but it ... to Lucy like a first marriage. When Maureen ... her about Bruce – her manner a shifty combination of exultation and embarrassment – Lucy ... . As soon as she ... him she ... at once that the long years of coping with Maureen's affairs ... over. Bruce ... manager of the branch of Tesco's at which Maureen herself ... – rather surprisingly – to supervisor. He had ... in some unspecified way by a wife who ... with an eight-year-old son and an immaculately equipped house in Cheam. Lucy ... that he ... entirely reliable and luxuriously in love with her mother.

Penelope Lively, *Cleopatra's Sister*.

to betray - to meet - to feel - to amaze - to remarry - to be (three times) - to get married - to rise - to tell - to see - to leave - to perceive

"Time" and "tense"

◆ *Faites bien la différence : "time" désigne le temps, notion physique ; "tense" désigne le temps grammatical.*

1 In the following paragraph, pick out the verbs which describe a past situation / action.

Dragons have been described in art and myth for thousands of years. They appear remarkably similar to certain dinosaurs. Is this coincidence ?
It is incorrectly assumed that the first dinosaur fossils were discovered during the last century. As long as humans have been walking the planet, they must have come across dinosaur skeletons.
Since the concept of extinction of species was unknown until relatively recently, it is easy to see how people deduced that fossilised bones of monsters belonged to a still living species.

2 C In the following paragraphs, pick out the verbs describing actions which happened before another past action or situation.

a. As we came to the end of the town, the sun had just gone down behind the river, and – I remember it as though it were yesterday – in the yellow sunset there was a sickle of new moon, and high over our heads a sprinkling of stars just coming dimly out. We stopped and looked.   C. P. Snow.

b. Ellen leaned back in the taxi and closed her eyes for a second. Not even the bath and the half-hour's nap had washed out the fagging memory of the office, the smell of it... She felt very tired ; she must have rings under her eyes. The taxi had stopped. There was a red light in the traffic tower ahead. Fifth avenue was jammed...

John Dos Passos.

3 **C** Pick out the verbal forms which give an indication about the time of the action.

Some sociologists say that full employment would be achieved if we all chose to work for 31.5 hours.

I read in some works of the classics that the oldest joke is recorded in graffiti at Pompeii. "How would you like your hair cut ?" "In silence."

The middle Americans cherish, apprehensively, a system of values that they see assaulted and mocked everywhere. "This," they will say with an air of embarrassment, "is the greatest country in the world. Why are people trying to tear it down ?".

Time Magazine.

4 **C** Trouvez le point commun de chacun des groupes d'énoncés suivants. Expliquez brièvement les différences à l'intérieur de chaque groupe.

1. **a.** Why are you reading my paper ?
   b. I'm playing tennis with him tomorrow.
   c. He's always playing the guitar !

2. **a.** He never drinks coffee.
   b. She's a teacher.
   c. He used to drive a Jaguar.
   d. You're always making the same mistake !
   e. You'll get used to it !

3. **a.** School starts on Monday.
   b. I'll call her tonight.
   c. I'm going to think about it.
   d. The plane is about to take off.
   e. The train is due to leave at 4 p.m.

4. **a.** I wish I had known him better.
   b. He talked to her as if she were a child.
   c. It's time you told her about it.

5. **a.** He'll probably arrive tomorrow.
   b. She's likely to succeed.
   c. He can't be wrong.
   d. They must have missed the train.
   e. It might rain.
   f. It's bound to happen.

Discours direct / discours indirect

1 **C** Transposez ce paragraphe au style direct.

One day in the middle of the twentieth century I sat in an old graveyard [...] when a young policeman stepped off the path and came over to me. He was shy and smiling [...] he only wanted to know what I was doing but plainly he didn't like to ask. I told him I was writing a poem, and offered him a sandwich which he refused as he had just had his dinner himself. He stopped to talk a while, then he said good-bye, the graves must be very old, and that he wished me good luck and that it was nice to speak to somebody.

Muriel Spark, *Loitering with Intent*.

2 Transposez au discours indirect.

♦ *La difficulté de cet exercice réside moins dans le problème de la concordance des temps que dans le choix du verbe d'introduction du discours indirect. Vous serez peut-être amené(e) à supprimer une partie (tag par exemple) de la phrase de départ. Il vous faudra compenser cette perte en employant le verbe approprié, en faisant appel aux fonctions de communication sous forme de verbes.*
Exemple : "Happy New Year !" → He wished me a happy New Year.
"Oh, I see, thank you !" → He seemed to have understood (contenu dans Oh, I see) and thanked me.

- "Be careful !"
- "I can't cope with such a problem."
- "Don't worry, I'm sure you'll do better next time."
- "You haven't got a pen-knife, have you ?"
- "I tell you what : we'll go to the restaurant."
- "It has to get there by the 30th ? Well, send it by air."
- "He's got the job !" "You don't say !"
- "He's passed." "Hey, that's terrific !"
- "You're expected to come !" "Oh, no !"
- "Excuse me. Do you know how I can get from here to Heathrow Airport ?"

3 Transposez ce passage du style direct libre au style indirect. Apportez les modifications nécessaires.

The telephone rang. It was Sally, to thank me. She and Kate have been talking about my offer, and have decided to come to some sort of arrangement, provided I really mean it.
Of course I mean it. I only wish I could afford to do more.
Don't be silly. Sally's voice sounds tearful. You've done everything. Where

would either of us be without you ? I just hope I can do as well for my two. I can hear her sniffing quite loudly now.
Of course you will.
And to change the subject I told her about my leaking roof, and the flooding down in the valley.

Eva Figes, *The Seven Ages*.

4 Après avoir lu très attentivement ce passage, réécrivez l'ensemble du texte sous forme de dialogue. Utilisez le moins possible les verbes to say et to tell.

He wanted to go to Mars on the rocket. He went down to the rocket field in the early morning and yelled in through the wire fence at the men in uniform that he wanted to go to Mars. He told them he was a taxpayer, his name was Pritchard, and he had a right to go to Mars. Wasn't he born right here in Ohio ? Wasn't he a good citizen ? Then why couldn't he go to Mars ? He shook his fists at them and told them that he wanted to get away from Earth, anybody with any sense wanted to get away from Earth. There was going to be a big atomic war on Earth in about two years, and he didn't want to be here when it happened. He and thousands of others like him, if they had any sense, would go to Mars. To get away from wars and censorship and statism and conscription and government control of this and that, of art and science ! He was offering his good right hand, his heart, for the opportunity to go to Mars ! What did you have to do, what did you have to sign, whom did you have to know, to get on the rocket ?
They laughed out through the wire screen at him. He didn't want to go to Mars, they said. Didn't he know that the First and Second Expeditions had failed, had vanished ; the men were probably dead ?
But they couldn't prove it, they didn't know for sure, he said, clinging to the wire fence. Maybe it was a land of milk and honey up there, and Captain York and Captain Williams had just never bothered to come back. Now were they going to open the gate and let him in to board the Third Expeditionary Rocket, or was he going to have to kick it down ?
They told him to shut up.
He saw the men walking out to the rocket.
Wait for me ! he cried. Don't leave me here on this terrible world, I've got to get away ; there's going to be an atom war ! Don't leave me on Earth ! They dragged him, struggling, away. They slammed the police wagon door and drove him off into the early morning, his face pressed to the rear window, and just before they sirened over a hill, he saw the red fire and heard the big sound and felt the huge tremor as the silver rocket shot up and left him behind on an ordinary Monday morning on the ordinary planet Earth.

Ray Bradbury, *The Martian Chronicles*.

3 LA PHRASE

Tags

Find a sentence corresponding to the tag.

..........................., shouldn't there ?
..........................., could you ?
..........................., can't we ?
..........................., shall we ?
..........................., doesn't she ?
..........................., will you ?
..........................., didn't they ?
..........................., have you ?
..........................., was there ?
..........................., is it ?

Place de l'adverbe

1 C Insert the adverbs in a correct place in the following sentences.

Until now, special effects in Indian cinema have been amateurish. (*mostly*)
Film makers have been turning to high-tech computers to give their films a fantastic feel. (*however / lately*)

Most experienced travellers keep seat belts fastened during flight for extra comfort in case of unexpected turbulence. (*usually / loosely*)

We would like to remind you to keep your hand-baggage secure under your seat or stored in the overhead lockers. (*also / safely*)

"I considered the possibility that I would not emerge from prison one day. I thought that a life sentence meant life and that I would die behind bars… I knew that some day I would feel the grass under my feet and walk in the sunshine a free man." (*never seriously / never / truly / always / once again*)

Nelson Mandela.

2 Put the adverbs in the correct place in the sentence, making the necessary arrangements.

1. Stephen was something of a legend – a gifted and brilliant musician. (*already / exceptionally*)

2. I was terribly pleased to hear his voice on the phone. (*always*)
3. People ask what we find to talk about. (*often*)
4. We saw each other last year because of work. (*hardly*)
5. Jamie took a picture of us which looked just as if we were getting married, yet we were only at the having tea stage. (*still*)
6. The extent to which you can personalise your own space in the office corresponds to your place in the hierarchy. (*usually*)
7. Last weekend we visited some friends who moved to North Oxfordshire. (*recently*)
8. Whether or not you like this cream seems a question of individual taste. (*very much*)
9. They have been married for two months. (*only*)

Formes interrogatives

You get a long distance telephone call. Unfortunately, you can't hear very clearly. Fill in the missing words and complete the conversation using the following interrogative pronouns :
what – how long – when – how – who – where.

Hello, is this 242 00 76 ?
Yes it is.
This is … speaking.
Jane Stewart, I'm calling from … .
Sorry, you're calling from … ?
San Diego, California…

Prépositions et particules

C Complete with the appropriate particles.

Ethical investments
Getting a good return …… your savings is a high priority if you invest money, but what if you're profiting …… activities you don't approve …… ? …… your pension, or personal equity plan, you could be investing …… a company that carries …… laboratory tests …… animals, sells arms …… countries …… a poor human rights record or a company whose waste pollutes our country's rivers.

According ...... a Mintel survey, one ...... three ...... us would invest ethically even if it meant a lower return. Although a growing number of investment funds now take ethical considerations ...... account when investing your money, not all are as pure as they claim. A recent report ...... *Which ?* showed that ...... 17 ethical funds none were ethical ...... every respect.

The rebirth of Glyndebourne
Glyndebourne is a legend ...... the world ...... opera – but sadly ...... scores of opera lovers, it has never been more than that. The little opera house has been packed season ...... season and, ... friends and sponsors had exercised their priority booking, the general public was lucky to get a look .... Good news, then, that the new and much larger theatre opens this year – and ...... prices well ...... the average.

Woman and Home Magazine, June 1994.

Multiples points de grammaire

1 C Réécrivez ces phrases sans en changer le sens.
1. What fun it had been to arrange their living-room !
2. How lucky it was that they should understand each other so well !
3. Isn't your baby beautiful ?
4. You've certainly grown !
5. That's nice !
6. She was such a good and non-stop reader !

2 C Complete the following sentences.
1. If you stand on one of the hills which overlook the city ... .
2. This book is designed to give you practice in ... .
3. No one knows yet ... .
4. 25 years ago ... .
5. If you had bought the January edition of *Time* you ... .
6. She told me ... .
7. I don't feel like ... .
8. It's high time ... .
9. We'll go to the museum when ... .
10. While the guests were dancing ... .

3 Complete the following sentences.

◆ *Nous attirons votre attention sur les éléments pertinents au plan grammatical en les soulignant.*

1. In the <u>last</u> two years ... .
2. The police accused him <u>of</u> ... .
3. He <u>warned</u> her ... .
4. I'd enjoy living here <u>if</u> ... .
5. They <u>wish</u> they ... .
6. <u>I'll</u> help you with your <u>work as soon as</u> ... .
7. She wondered <u>why</u> ... .
8. I'll let you know <u>as soon as</u> ... .
9. We suggested <u>that</u> the money ... .
10. On August 16th <u>he was presented</u> to the press and ... <u>ever since</u>.

4 Complete the following sentences.

1. He was the first man ... .
2. It's no good ... .
3. The doctor has advised him ... .
4. You'll feel better when ... .
5. If you had come ... .
6. I hate washing up. I'd much rather you ... .
7. He changed his name so that ... .
8. ... when I heard a knock on the door.
9. Wouldn't it be better ... .
10. The shopkeeper asked ... .

5 C Rewrite the following sentences using the starters provided.

1. She thought : "It makes no difference". *She thought that ... any ...* .
2. I've never seen such an exciting film. *It's the most ...* .
3. "I'll feel better, then, I'll move." "When I ...". *She said that when ...* .
4. He looked at me ; I looked at him. *We ...* .
5. "Could I have a drink, please ?" " *... mind ...* ".
6. "You'd better turn it off," he said. *He ...* .
7. It's three years since I last saw him. *I haven't ...* .
8. I didn't go, she didn't go either. *... neither ...* .
9. He insisted that I should sell the house. *He insisted on ...* .

6 Rewrite the following sentences using the starters.

1. It is possible to argue forever. *You* ... .
2. He suggested giving her a bottle of perfume. *He said* ... .
3. You can't speak of the problems of Northern Ireland unless you know its history well. *If* ... .
4. Since 1902 every Prime Minister has been a member of the House of Commons. ... *for* ... .
5. People are spending far more money on clothes now than they spent years ago. *Far more money* ... .
6. I told her to stop making a fuss about nothing. *I said* ... .
7. Never wear a pair of jeans until you've washed them at least five times. *You* ... .
8. She asked me if I had watched TV on Sunday. *She asked* ... .
9. Should you care to give your doggie a birthday party, the Animal Gourmet will gladly cater the affair. *If* ... .
10. "Fasten your seat-belts," said the air hostess. *The hostess* ... .
11. Perspiration was streaming from his face, yet he made no move to open his shirt. *Although* ... .
12. "Don't smoke near the petrol pump," the mechanic said. *The mechanic* ... .

7 Reformulez chaque énoncé sans en modifier le sens :
a. à l'aide de l'amorce imposée,
b. par une phrase à votre convenance.

1. Marjorie, is there anything the matter with you ?
   a. ...... *wrong* ....   b. ......
2. Old as they were, her aunts also did their share of the housework.
   a. *Although* ......   b. ......
3. It was long after ten o'clock and yet there was no sign of Gabriel.
   a. *Despite* ......   b. ......
4. Kate nearly doubled herself so heartily did she enjoy the joke.
   a. ...... *so much that* ....   b. ......
5. If I were you I'd take some riding lessons.
   a. ...... *should* ....   b. ......
6. He advised us to read this article.
   a. *He suggested* ....   b. ......

7. I'm sorry she didn't stay for the party.
   a. *I wish* ....   b. ......
8. It's a long time since we last went to Canada.
   a. *We haven't* ....   b. ......
9. If he doesn't apologize I will never speak to him again.
   a. *Unless* ....   b. ......
10. Phoning the police was not necessary.
    a. *You* ....   b. ......

8 C Read the following paragraphs carefully, then answer the questions.

The bus-stop, just as in the old days, was the area of pavement outside the *Mairie*. This florid building was now painted salmon pink, no longer the faded grey that Thérèse remembered. She shrugged, watching the bus depart, backside of blue gas farting exhaust. She stooped to pick up her bags. [...]
She crossed the road, to take the turning that led off between the chemist's and the blacksmith's. Oh. There was no longer a blacksmith's. And the chemist's window, which used to contain antique apothecary pots in *vieux Rouen* porcelain, was now full of strip-lit placards of naked women scrubbing their thighs with green mittens. [...] Thérèse walked on.
She told herself that she was calm. That she was on the right road. That her feet did recognize its bends and loops. There was a pavement now, streetlamps and bus-shelters on this stretch, signs warning of sharp corners, an old people's home. The old school had been knocked down and a new one, prefab style, built in its place next to an asphalt playground. Only half a kilometer on did the countryside as she remembered it burst upon her.
                                        Michèle Roberts, *Daughters of the House*.

C 1. List the expressions showing that Thérèse is coming back to a place she once knew well.

2. What are the tenses used to describe the changes that have taken place.

3. Write a paragraph using these expressions to describe your school (street, etc.) as it used to be and as it is now.

4. *That her feet did recognize its bends and loops.* (l. 11 - 12). Explain the use of *did* in this sentence. Write three mini dialogues using a similar grammatical form.

EXPRESSION

1. MÉTHODE

RÉDIGER UN DIALOGUE **92**
ÉCRIRE UNE LETTRE **93**
TRAITER UN SUJET DE RÉFLEXION **94**
- ANALYSER L'ÉNONCÉ D'UN SUJET **94**
- TROUVER DES ARGUMENTS **96**
- FAIRE UN PLAN **98**
- RÉDIGER UNE INTRODUCTION **99**
- ORGANISER SES IDÉES **101**

2. FONCTIONS DE COMMUNICATION

COMPARAISON, CONTRASTE **102**
DEGRÉS DE PROBABILITÉ **103**
CONSEIL **107**
CAUSE, CONSÉQUENCE, BUT **108**
APPROBATION, DÉSAPPROBATION **108**

3. RÉDACTION

CONSTRUIRE DES PHRASES **110**
RÉDIGER DES PARAGRAPHES **113**
EMPLOYER LES MOTS DE LIAISON **116**

4. SUJETS DE RÉDACTION **118**

1 MÉTHODE

Rédiger un dialogue

◆ *Quand on rédige un dialogue, il ne suffit pas de rapporter les paroles des différents personnages. Il faut aussi donner des indications sur leur ton, leur état d'esprit, leur psychologie...*

1 Lisez le dialogue suivant et soulignez les expressions qui donnent ce type d'indications.

On a dank August afternoon, Howard picked up an ammonite on Blue Anchor beach.
He presented it to his parents. "What's this ?"
"It's a stone," said his father, who was listening to the test match.
"No, it isn't," retorted Howard, an observant child.
"It's a fossil, dear," said his mother. "That's a very old sort of stone."
[...]
During the rest of the afternoon, he collected five more fossil fragments, including one embedded in a slab of rock weighing several pounds.
His parents expostulated. There were already the picnic basket, the folding chairs, the radio, the beach bag, the ball, the cricket stumps. "Any of those stones you want to take back you're carrying yourself, do you understand ?" instructed his father.
"They're not stones," the child protested.

Penelope Lively, *Cleopatra's Sister*.

2 Depending on the tone a sentence can have different meanings. Classify the following sentences according to their possible meaning (you may tick more than one), then choose one and add the adequate verbs and/or adverbs.

reproach - anger - refusal - shock - threat - suspicion - doubt - lack of enthusiasm - excuse - statement

1. "And why precisely were you moving the filing cabinet for Carol ? Surely she could have got one of the students to do that ?"...
2. "Write for newspapers !" ...
3. "This must be a government building of some kind." ...
4. "For Christ's sake !" ... "We've had enough of this !" ...
5. "Dr Greeley will see you now." ...

6. "I'll have you know I'm not used to being addressed in this fashion !" …
7. "I couldn't possibly wait for the next train, I'm afraid." …
8. "Yes…, if you want to, Jim." …
9. "Sorry, Noel. I'm still a bit tired. I just don't feel up to it yet. Still recovering from my journey, I think." …
10. "Mary !" … . "Why didn't you tell us you had valuables hidden in your room ! We might have been burgled ! This is gold, isn't it ?"

Écrire une lettre

◆ *Your address must be written in the top right-hand corner. Don't write your name there.*
◆ *Write the date under your address.*

Greetings	Endings
• to a stranger	
Dear Sirs, (to a company) *Dear Sir, Dear Madam,*	*Yours faithfully,*
• to someone you know or who has written to you	
Dear Mr X, Dear Mrs X, Dear Miss X,	*Yours sincerely,* *Yours,* *With kindest regards,*
• to someone you know quite well	
Dear Jane, My dear Peter, *My dear Mr L.,*	*With love from…* *Love from us all,* *Yours,* *All the best,*
• to someone who is very close to you	
Dear Bob, *My dearest Kate,* *My darling Clementine,*	*Love,* *Lots of love from…* *Much love, as always,* *xxxxxxx (= lots of kisses)*

The first sentence

Here are some examples of the way you can start a letter.
Thank you for your letter, which came this morning…
I am sorry I haven't written for so long…

How good it was to hear from you…
I am writing to ask whether…
This is to order…
In reply to your letter dated…
Would you please send me… I enclose my cheque for…

1 Write the letter to which the following is the answer.

> **TEXTILE HERITAGE COLLECTION**
> ALBERT STREET
> EDINBURGH
> SCOTLAND
>
> *Thank you for your enquiry regarding our kits.*
> *We do supply our kits mail order, price list enclosed.*
> *We also supply to a shop in Paris. The address is*
> *4 rue du Moulin Bleu.*
> *We hope this is of help to you.*
> *With compliments,*

2 Turn the following telegram into a letter.
Elizabeth. Sorry can't come. Hectic time. Sandra ill. New job. New address from July 1st : 11 Portland Street. Laramie, Wyo. Love. Paul.

Traiter un sujet de réflexion

ANALYSER L'ÉNONCÉ D'UN SUJET

◆ *La première démarche avant toute rédaction consiste à analyser ce qui est demandé.*

C Voici différents types de sujets possibles.

a. Récit/prise de position à partir d'une **expérience personnelle**.
Recall an experience in which you were led to **change your mind**.
b. Sujet d'**imagination.**
Imagine Mick's dream about the future.

c. Réponse à **une question** avec prise de position personnelle.
What, in your opinion, *should be the role of the artist in our modern society ?*

d. **Discussion** puis prise de position.
Does** the consumer society necessarily destroy our spiritual life **?

e. Expansion/**explication** d'une idée contenue ou non dans le texte. Prise de position personnelle.
In a 1927 interview, before his third attempt to conquer Mount Everest which was to cost him his life, Mallory was asked why he wanted so much to conquer that mountain. He simply replied : "Because it's there." **What, do you think, motivates** *people to risk their lives and is it worth taking such risks ?*

Classez les sujets suivants.
Soulignez les mots clés de la consigne.

	a	b	c	d	e
1. You have either read texts or seen films about the North American Indians. What have you learned about their lifestyles and culture ? In what ways do they stand so far apart from the ways of European and American developed countries ? Do you think that lessons might be learned from them ? In what fields ?					
2. "Unemployment is the plague of industrial societies". What is your position on this issue ?					
3. The English-speaking world : does a common language stand for a common culture ?					
4. Do you think that fox-hunting, like bull-fighting in Spain, should be maintained as a spectacular aspect of English traditions, or do you disapprove of this sport ?					
5. Which book has had the greatest impact on you so far ?					
6. Do you think modern education is adapted to the present times ? Are school-leavers well prepared to face the "struggle for life" ?					
7. Imagine the ideal workplace. To what extent can efficiency and pleasure combine ? Provide examples to support your arguments.					

	a	b	c	d	e
8. A newsphotographer's job is to "hold open the shutter when the world wants to close its eyes." (G. Swift). What is your personal opinion about the covering of human suffering by the media ?					
9. Advertising : a new form of art ?					
10. How do you imagine the best form of education ?					

TROUVER DES ARGUMENTS

■ Pour ou contre ? Classez les arguments suivants dans la catégorie adéquate. Soulignez les mots ou expressions clés. Trouvez pour chaque sujet un argument pour ou contre supplémentaire.

1. This Christmas, parents will spend up to £300m on computer games for their children. Are they wasting their money ?

Arguments	For	Against
Playing computer games, it is said, rots a child's mind quicker than glue-sniffing. With persistent looped music and repetitive screen displays, it may be a slower process, but it is just as addictive. Add to that the violent male-dominated imagery in some games and there seems to be a huge potential for harm.		
Those same computer games that so concern their parents are in fact the secret recruiting ground for the computer generation. For not only does playing games provide astonishing education in perception and problem-solving, it also leads to an easy familiarity with computers that is entirely lacking the parents.		
The computer is a kind of cyberspace for the cultivation of knowledge at a child's own pace and discretion.		
Experience has shown that a computer is no real substitute for a living teacher.		

2. England Hit by Lottery Fever !

Arguments

I do not like the sight of adult human beings I know and respect dribbling in front of the television screen because they think they are going to win £6m.

The reason why I won't buy a single lottery ticket is that I know I'm not going to win and my ego can't take it.

We all want there to be such a thing as free money.

	For	Against

3. The private ownership of guns in the U. S.

Arguments

In the United States accidental and intentional deaths due to guns in and around the home are commonplace in most major cities, and a substantial proportion of an entire generation of young people are armed and prepared to shoot with little or no provocation.

"As a Governor, I'm concerned with crime protection and Oregon's penal system. And like other NRA[1] members I want guns to be used safely and legally. We believe strict punishment is the best solution to crime with a gun."

1. National Rifle Association

Survey of gun owners indicates that they believe guns protect them from intruders.

There's a nearly fivefold increase of suicide in homes where guns are kept.

"I look at the eighty guns in my collection and wonder 'Who owned them ?', 'Who shot them ?' They kind of hook me up with history and make the days of George Washington, Lincoln and the pioneers much more real than the pages of a history book ever could."

	For	Against

FAIRE UN PLAN

◆ *Selon le type de sujet, vous pouvez adopter plusieurs techniques. Si l'énoncé implique le développement d'idées opposées, vous pouvez envisager thèse, antithèse et synthèse.*
Pour développer une prise de position personnelle, vous pouvez :
– analyser les composants de l'énoncé, puis donner des exemples,
– énoncer les faits, puis les causes et les conséquences.

1 Choisissez le type de plan qui convient à votre avis aux sujets suivants.

1. It appears that watching TV has replaced reading books for many teenagers. Comment on this statement, giving your opinion.

2. "The State and not the families should provide for the needs of the elderly." Discuss.

3. In history there have been examples of extremely rich people who found it their duty to help fellow-men, especially artists, with their money. Do you know of such wealthy patrons ?

2 Voici un plan détaillé. Étudiez-le attentivement, puis rédigez l'énoncé de la question posée.

Introduction
The moral status of animals has been the subject of intense discussion.

Part 1
According to some authors, animals shouldn't be used as research subjects because…
– Opinion 1 : "animals have rights similar to those of human beings."
– Opinion 2 : they have no rights but "it violates their interest in avoiding suffering".

Part 2
In stark contrast other authors consider that the use of animals as research subjects is justified.
– Opinion 1 : animals may have some rights but not the right not to be used for research.
– Opinion 2 : animals have no rights and can be used as experimental subjects.

Conclusion
This debate has had two consequences.
– A reevaluation of the goals and methods of biomedical research.
– A new awareness of the moral implications of the use of animals.

3 Sur le même modèle, rédigez un plan sur le sujet suivant.

Do you think there should be limits to the freedom of the press ? Illustrate with examples taken from the British and American press.

RÉDIGER UNE INTRODUCTION

◆ *L'introduction permet de situer le sujet. C'est une présentation, une mise en perspective générale ou particulière.*
*Le **choix d'un temps** particulier est un facteur essentiel d'une telle rédaction. Il sera également utile de **bien définir** les termes du sujet.*
***Poser une ou des questions** peut être une transition intéressante avec le développement.*

1 Le choix d'un temps

Présent continu (**be +** base verbale -*ing*)	Représente un « arrêt sur image» Dirige l'attention sur un fait actuel.
Present perfect	Temps du bilan.
Présent simple	Aborde les faits sans commentaire. Film de l'action présente.
Prétérit	Temps de la narration. Insistance sur l'action passée.

Analysez les choix effectués par les auteurs dans la première phrase de l'article écrit.

1. *The Post Yuppie Generation*
They have trouble making decisions. They would rather hike in the Himalayas than climb the corporate ladder. They have few heroes, no anthems, no style to call their own. They crave entertainment, but their attention span is as short as one zap of a TV dial. They hate yuppies, hippies and druggies. They postpone marriage because they dread divorce.

2. *The Race against Crime*
Specially-trained units of the Hong Kong police are cracking down on one of the city's worst plagues : triads or secret crime societies…

3. *Refugees in Seattle*
Since the 1970s, over three million Asian immigrants have arrived in the USA. Many of their children have succeeded brilliantly in school, but others have had a difficult time adjusting to life in America.

4. Annals of Crime
Mike left the airport in the car he had stolen. Somewhere, he stopped and bent part of the rear license plate back on itself, to conceal the number...

2 Comment s'organise l'introduction de l'article ci-dessous ?

What is the good death ?
It is the scene modern man dreads. He is in a hospital, desperately ill and alone. By his side is a respirator, supplementing his breathing with a regular sigh of its own. Tubes run into his nose and stomach, carrying fluids that keep him alive. As death approaches, he has lost control of his life. Modern medicine affords marvellous cures ; it keeps men and women alive longer than they could have hoped for even half a century ago. Yet, when life is prolonged, there is all the more chance that it will end in debilitation, dementia and dependence. The old used to be snatched away by pneumonia, "the old man's friend" ; or by a heart attack ; now pneumonia can be cured with antibiotics, and stopped hearts can be pounded back to life with cardio-pulmonary resuscitation. Man can cheat death.
But the cheating brings with it a crowd of questions. Should people be kept alive who, without intervention, would surely die ? Should patients be allowed to choose for themselves whether or not to go on living ? Should doctors become ministers, not of cures, but of easeful death ? How are life, and death, to be valued ?
The Economist, July 20, 1991.

3 Rédigez les deux ou trois premières phrases d'introduction aux sujets suivants.

◆ *Dans un premier temps, définissez clairement la tâche qui vous est donnée (devez-vous faire un récit, comparer, donner une opinion, imaginer, décrire, émettre des hypothèses ?).*

1. Do you consider you were happier when you were twelve years old ?

2. If you were a journalist, which field would most appeal to you (foreign affairs, home affairs, fashion, music and arts, sports) ?

3. "If ecologists had their way, most people would be unemployed." Do you agree ?

4. Recall an experience in which you were led to change your mind about a person or about a place.

5. Some people assert "where there is a will, there is a way". Comment and illustrate.

ORGANISER SES IDÉES

◆ Un paragraphe pour être intéressant doit être le **développement d'une idée** principale. Énoncez celle-ci au début du paragraphe, puis explicitez-la à l'aide d'exemples et enfin concluez ou assurez une transition vers une autre idée.

◆ Pensez à employer des mots de liaison afin d'étayer votre développement.

Pour énumérer
first / to start with / finally / lastly / eventually / next / then

Pour faire une digression/ajouter
incidentally / what's more / not only… but also / furthermore

Pour exprimer une cause/donner un exemple
for instance / for example / namely / that is to say
the reason why / since (puisque) / given that

Pour exprimer une conséquence
therefore / consequently / as a result
owing to / on account of / because of + groupe nominal

Pour conclure
to sum up / to conclude / in conclusion / in short / in brief

Pour faire une transition
to turn to / as for / now

■ Reprenez le plan que vous avez choisi pour l'un des sujets, page 98.

■ Répertoriez les mots de liaison qui vous seront utiles pour passer d'une phrase à l'autre ou d'un paragraphe à l'autre.

FONCTIONS DE COMMUNICATION

◆ *Les exercices qui vont suivre sont destinés à enrichir votre expression par un travail systématique sur les fonctions de communication.*

Comparaison, contraste

1 Read the following sentences and underline the expressions of comparison.

1. We set out to build the best small car in the world.
2. X… has eight inches more rear seat hip room than Z…
3. The W… is the best blend of innovation, economy, and fun-to-drive we have seen in almost a decade.
4. A rousing welcome from the Z… island that stands for the happiest of vacations.
5. The credit for such a high degree of comfort must go to the P…'s shock absorbers, which contain four times as many valves as normal shock absorbers.
6. Arguably the most comfortable car in existence today.
7. The lightest, smoothest liquid ink pen with unique cushioned ball tip.
8. Unbeatable ! X… still fastest East.
9. Say more than "cheese".
10. Box : less than 0.5 mg "tar", 0.05 mg nicotine per cigarette.

Now make at least five sentences on the same pattern.

2 Vous trouverez dans la colonne de gauche des débuts de phrases dont les fins se trouvent à droite. Retrouvez les phrases complètes. Relevez les procédés employés pour exprimer la comparaison ou le contraste.

a. I'm 47 years old	1. matters have improved.
b. Unlike J. Kennedy in her White House years	2. faster than any single-hulled sailboat, about twice as fast as 65-foot yachts.
c. Like the eyes	3. ,this one concentrates on politics.

d. Despite its small size	4. , and I cannot tell anybody where I have been or what I have been doing all my life.
e. It's fashionable	5. but in hard times split up.
f. Though they have a sign that reads "equal opportunity kitchen" over the sink	6. ,this camera uses standard 35 mm film.
g. Coyotes will run in packs like wolves	7. the princess shops patriotically.
h. In a stiff breeze a fiber glass sailboard can go	8. , the only chore Nelson performs is cooking bacon and eggs for breakfast.
i. Time stops :	9. these lenses change as the light changes.
j. X cooking products give you	10. without being a fad.
k. During the past 20 years, however	11. better meals, less work and like all our appliances are backed by our 24 hour service.
l. While his first novel was about everything under the sun	12. : it's like floating, flying.

Comparing	Contrasting
Example : *like ... -ing* (12)	*, and* (4)
....	.... I...
....	....

◆ *Complétez ces listes au fil de vos lectures avec d'autres expressions du contraste ou de la comparaison.*

Degrés de probabilité

1 C Are the facts written *in italics* considered as certain, possible or probable by the writer or the speaker ?

1. *The traditional cultures are*, in any case, *doomed*.
2. If we are lucky we may eventually *arrive at a totally integrated world culture*.

3. The noise problem that probably *leads to a more widespread irritation* than any other is domestic or neighbour noise. When your neighbours next throw a rowdy party, it is not much use calling the police because they may not *come* unless you can *convince them* there is likely *to be a breach of the peace.*

4. In 2020 both books and publications will *become much cheaper* and therefore available in far greater variety. I see no reason why we should not *have scores of national daily newspapers*, and of course we shall be able to *summon up the pages of the New York Times and the Sydney Morning Herald* by dialing the right code.

5. There may well *be many dead pulsars moving through space.* We may be sure that *there are no such objects in the Solar System but* sooner or later it is possible that we will *encounter one of them.*

6. It is possible *to foresee the loss* of thousands of plant and animal species while at the same time the air we breathe, the water we drink and the soil in which we grow our food *becomes ever more polluted.*

7. If they do not agree, they will just have *to take the consequences*, which might ultimately *be fatal.*

8. We will *be freed to devote ourselves to creative pursuits, able to educate our children in the arts and sciences.* In this new golden age, we will *start* our real exploration of the universe.

9. However much a commercial costs to make, it will almost certainly *be less than the cost of showing it.* T.V. advertising can *cost anything from £300 to £30.000* for 30 seconds.

10. It is quite possible that by 2020 there will *be manned bases on the Moon.*

2 Write a paragraph about what you consider as certain, probable and possible in 2095.

3 Your Stars

Virgo (Aug 24 - Sept 22) : You will be sorry to start your working week because you are not feeling too good. A friend at work may invite you out. You may be brooding over some minor problem.

Libra (Sept 23 - Oct. 23) : A pleasant but uneventful day. You will hear some gossip which isn't true. Friends may keep you busy on the phone. You are feeling stand-offish in a romance and won't be taken for granted.

Scorpio (Oct 24 - Nov 22) : Your sweetheart may get jealous. Perhaps you are appearing to give too much love to someone else. You may mislay something of value.

Sagittarius (Nov 23 - Dec 21) : Travel will be difficult and you may have to go by another route. A sweetheart could be hiding something from you, but this isn't the best time to pry. A bit of make believe is fun tonight.

Capricorn (Dec 22 - Jan 20) : You'll need a touch of glamour so buy something to make you look marvellous. Capricorn men feel dignified, Capricorn women are longing to be wooed ! Let's hope you are not disappointed.

Aquarius (Jan 21 - Feb 18) : There is no time for day-dreaming. You are in the mood for fun, but your partner isn't. An item in the news will arouse your anger.

Pisces (Feb 19 - March 20) : Quite a lucky day. You could have more than one winner. If you are trying to impress people on the off chance, you'll score a surprising success. Don't be late for an appointment.

Aries (March 21 - April 20) : It looks like a busy day. Friends may drop by and arrange something for next weekend. A chore may take longer than you think. If you are courting, you won't have much time to yourself.

Taurus (April 21 - May 21) : As soon as a quarrel breaks out, look on the funny side of life. If you have a bad tempered partner, you will soon love him or her out of a black mood. But a practical joke will misfire.

Gemini (May 22 - June 21) : You must be thrifty in one way but can splurge out somewhere else. If you are in love, you may be disappointed for a while – then everything turns out fine. Good links with Libran folks.

Cancer (June 22 - July 22) : There is a lot of fun to be had – at someone else's expense. Links with another country are strong at present – so it's a good time to write or make an international call.

Leo (July 23 - Aug 23) : There could be a disappointment at work, but there are several compensations. The family will be in an argumentative mood and children won't do what you want !

The Sun.

---

1. Among the following speech-functions which can be found in this horoscope ?

☐ Warning ☐ Order ☐ Appreciation ☐ Suggestion
☐ Advice ☐ Probability ☐ Complaint

2. List the expressions of probability and classify them according to their degree of probability.

3. What subjects are not mentioned ?

☐ Romance ☐ Politics ☐ Health ☐ Luck
☐ Work   ☐ Family   ☐ Friends ☐ Weather

4. Paragraph writing
- With the help of questions 1, 2, 3 invent a horoscope for one sign.
- Do you often read your horoscope ?
- Do you know people who do so ? Why do they do it ?

■■■■■■■ Conseil

■ Study the document carefully. Underline the different ways of formulating the instructions and the link-words.

Write out a similar set of instructions, or advice.

Luck

At various times during your adventure, either in battles or when you come across situations in which you could either be lucky or unlucky (details of these are given on the pages themselves), you may call on your luck to make the outcome more favourable. But beware! Using luck is a risky business and if you are *un*lucky, the results could be disastrous.

The procedure for using your luck is as follows : roll two dice. If the number rolled is *equal to or less than* your current LUCK score, you have been *lucky* and the result will go in your favour. If the number rolled is *higher* than your current LUCK score, you have been *unlucky* and you will be penalized.

This procedure is known as *Testing your Luck*. Each time you *Test your Luck*, you must substract one point from your current LUCK score. Thus you will soon realize that the more you rely on your luck, the more risky this will become.

Using Luck in Battles

On certain pages of the book you will be told to *Test your Luck* and will be told the consequences of your being *lucky* or *unlucky*. However, in battles, you always have the *option* of using your luck either to inflict a more serious wound on a creature you have just wounded, or to minimize the effects of a wound the creature has just inflicted on you.

If you have just wounded the creature, you may *Test your Luck* as described above. If you are *lucky*, you have inflicted a severe wound and may substract an *extra* 2 points from the creature's STAMINA score. However, if you are *unlucky*, the wound was a mere graze and you must restore 1 point to the creature's STAMINA (i. e. instead of scoring the normal 2 points of damage, you have now scored only 1).

If the creature has just wounded you, you may *Test your Luck* to try to minimize the wound. If you are *lucky*, you have managed to avoid the full damage of the blow. Restore 1 point of STAMINA (i. e. instead of doing 2 points of damage it has done only 1). If you are *unlucky*, you have taken a more serious blow. Substract 1 extra STAMINA point.

Remember that you must substract 1 point from your own LUCK score each time you *Test your Luck*.

Steve Jackson, *The Citadel of Chaos*

Cause, conséquence, but

Dans les phrases suivantes, soulignez les mots utilisés pour exprimer la cause, la conséquence, le but. Reformulez ensuite ces mêmes phrases en employant d'autres procédés.

1. A couple of nights, we rented a motel room so the kids would stay here.

2. Each sumptuous volume will be strikingly different from the others… Thus, when the complete collection is arranged in the owner's home, its variety will fire the imagination.

3. Though rabies is a genuine threat to animals and humans, scare stories can be threatening and lead to overreaction against wild animals.

4. They have spent a year in a Cuban jail for trying to smuggle marijuana.

5. It's not something that we think about a lot because we do have very demanding responsibilities.

6. In order to illuminate this growing national problem, *Life* here examines these children's pitiful lot.

7. Florida's celebrated swamps face the loss of their quintessential element : water… As a result, the population of wading birds has dwindled by 90%.

8. I love the unexpected, and that's why she gave me a gift I'll never forget.

9. The words "limbs" and "waist" were used in strange ways by nineteenth century American ladies. This was caused by their desire to avoid talking about impolite subjects.

10. The purpose of this article is to examine the characteristics of video and see what it can do for us more effectively.

Approbation, désapprobation

Vous trouverez ci-contre des extraits d'un certain nombre de lettres adressées à un journal. Les lecteurs y expriment leur approbation, leur désapprobation, leur surprise, leur reconnaissance, après la lecture d'un article qui vient d'être publié.

1. Relevez les fonctions de communication.
2. Relevez les moyens employés correspondant à chaque fonction.
3. Écrivez un paragraphe sur le même sujet mais en contradiction totale avec celui que vous avez lu et analysé.

◆ Exemple

I'm furious. As a journalism teacher who spent four and a half years in Samoa, I found your report extremely sensationalized.
1. Indignation.
2. Furious, I found... sensationalized...
3. "I'm delighted. As a journalism teacher who spent four years in Samoa I found your report extremely truthful."

1. "Congratulations. I have always loved Moore's sculpture, but never so much as I did seeing it in your magazine."

2. "I find the National Survival Game absolutely revolting."

3. "I was really pleased to see your magazine put its name behind such a forceful article."

4. "Thanks for the article about national park abuse. It's about time this little-known crisis received cover-story notice."

5. "The article is grossly misleading to the American public and misrepresents the attitude of American fishermen toward foreign fishermen."

6. "After reading such a touching article I had a feeling of overwhelming compassion."

7. "With virtually no coverage given to the American fishing industry, I was shocked to see such valuable space in your magazine devoted to the 'detente' feature."

8. "Too bad your magazine didn't show America some true body building champions."

9. "After reading your article on the Texas prisons, I must say you have a misguided sense of right and wrong."

10. "Your article is biased, inaccurate and maliciously untrue."

11. "Three cheers for your article 'Baby in the Office'. I too am a working mother who has the honour and privilege of experiencing the best of both worlds. My thanks to those bosses who realize the importance of being both mother and provider."

12. "You were absolutely right in stating that T.G. is the main reason 14 million people watch General Hospital."

3 RÉDACTION

Construire des phrases

◆ *Vous trouverez ci-contre des phrases extraites de romans contemporains. Elles illustrent des constructions souvent délicates pour des francophones et qui sont à l'origine de nombreuses erreurs à l'examen.*

Étudiez bien ces phrases, puis dites pour chacune d'elles quel phénomène de langue elle illustre (plusieurs phénomènes peuvent être représentés dans la même phrase).

◆ *Faites cet exercice en plusieurs fois.*

Phénomène de langue	Phrases n°…
Accord	…
Accroissement parallèle	…
Adjectifs substantivés	…
Circonstancielles de temps	…
Différence entre *who* ? et *which* ?	…
Emploi de *both*	…
Emploi du gérondif / nom verbal	…
Emploi du subjonctif	…
Expression du souhait	…
Forme "emphatique"	…
Inversion hypothétique	…
it explétif	…
Ordre des compléments	…
Ordre des mots dans les phrases de style indirect	…
Phrases exclamatives	…
Place des adverbes de fréquence	…
Place de *enough*	…
Prétérit modal	…
Should et *would*	…
Traduction de "faire faire"	…
Traduction de "la plupart"	…

1. This morning she had begun listing the house contents in the inventory her lawyer had suggested she **draw up**.
2. I would suggest **you retire** for the night.
3. She looks into her closet : there isn't a lot of choice, and no matter what she wears, Roz will narrow her eyes at it and suggest **they go** shopping.
4. It was Roz who insisted **they go** on to the cemetery after the service.
5. Clifford insisted on **living** well, and also took pleasure in never spending a penny more than he had to do in so doing.

6. He **had a large custom-built studio built** at the end of the garden, disregarding the plea of the neighbours.
7. I knew that accidents bad **enough** to kill a man **usually** left their mark on a car. It was very strange.
8. I'm old **enough** to earn my own living, and to have a driving licence.
9. "Mother," said Clifford to Cynthia, on the Sunday morning, "what does father say about **my marrying** Helen ?"
"Why should he say anything ? You're old **enough** to know your own mind."
10. Catching sight of myself in the mirror-panelled wall, I decided that I would **never** wear this mouse-brown outfit again.
11. I had **often** suffered under his sarcasm.
12. It amused me to think I had a secret they would **never** know.
13. "You know my father's a spy ?"
"So you've told me," but Helen found **it** hard to believe.
14. It's hard to explain my feelings once I **did** finally set off.
15. Where are the paintings to be kept ? Yet if the painter **does** sell, and so makes room, it is like having a chunk of living flesh torn away.

16. "**I wish** you wouldn't burst in like that, Celia !" I snapped. "I've told you and told you to knock before you enter a lady's bedroom."
17. "**If only** you had been more tactful about it," said her mother, as near a reproach as she had ever uttered.
18. "I suppose you're right," he sighed. "I **wish** you weren't."
19. I **wish** I could say he became more tactful with the years, but he didn't.

20. "Angie," said Clifford, "I need to know exactly **who she is**."

21. "He left," said Angie, shortly.
"**Who with** ?"
"A girl."
"**Which** girl ?"
"**The one who** was wearing some kind of nightdress," said Angie.

22. "It's all your fault," she went on as he knew she **would**, before he could tell her **what the matter with her was**.

23. He thought **if only** he had married a different woman, how much happier **he would now be**.

24. It is surely unfair that youth and looks **should** seem to count more than wit, style, intelligence and experience.

25. He's going to be so upset **when he calms down** and finds out what he's done.

26. I think you **should** go next door and wait **till he calms down**.

27. **Most of us** can never quite get used to hurtling through the air, rather than crawling more reasonably over the ground ; and **the more** imagination we have, **the more** we project our scenarios of disasters ahead.

28. Now **the sooner** we get this right, **the sooner** we can all go home.

29. **What a** disagreeable man he was. **The more** I think of him **the more** disagreeable he gets.

30. **The more** the royals are seen as public benefactors **the less** of an issue their wealth would be.

31. He thought she was **both** the loveliest and the saddest woman he had ever seen.

32. You'll **both** feel better **once we've had** some exercise.

33. He liked a title ; he admired wealth ; he was flattered by the company of **the famous**.

34. **Had** the flight over the Channel been calm and placid the aircraft might well have got to Geneva safely.

35. **How lucky they are** to have you, Mrs Lee ; so warm and friendly and kind.

◆ *Exercez-vous à réutiliser ces constructions chaque fois que vous le pourrez. Complétez cette liste au fil de vos lectures. Vous enrichirez ainsi progressivement votre expression.*

Rédiger des paragraphes

◆ Il s'agit d'écrire un paragraphe en utilisant les éléments fournis, dans l'ordre, en ajoutant les mots manquants et en effectuant tous les changements nécessaires.

Veillez à la concordance des temps, aux mots de liaison, aux articles. Mettez la ponctuation.

1 C Write out the following outlines in complete sentences in the past tense.

- twenty-fifth / June / be / pleasant evening / unpleasant summer / I / just stroll home / enjoy it
- no hurry at all / just wonder / turn in / drink / somewhere / see / old man
- He / stand / pavement / Thanet Street / look unwell
- be late / every one / leave / café / except / old man / sit / window
- two waiters / know / old man / little drunk
- be / good client / they / know / he / become / too drunk / he / leave / without / pay

2 C Write out the following outlines beginning with the pluperfect.

- Andrew Mann / family / walk / picnic / fish / stream / time / go
- They / wait / bus / station
- it / expect / ten minutes
- wind / come up / sky / fill / dark / menacing / clouds
- Margaret / declare / Ann / need / holiday
- Ann / not be / out of England / fifteen years / Ann / see / France / Italy / again
- Ann / answered / Margaret / want / go / abroad / she / go / with / her

3 Lisez attentivement ces paragraphes, puis inventez-en de semblables en gardant les structures soulignées et en les adaptant bien sûr à vos nouvelles phrases.

◆ Cet exercice est difficile. Entraînez-vous d'abord sur certaines phrases.

C 1. <u>Since</u> Mrs Harris was <u>not</u> sports-minded <u>nor</u> had the time to follow the fortunes of the football teams, <u>and since as well</u> the possible combinations and permutations ran into the millions, she was <u>accustomed to making</u> out her selections by guess and by God.   Paul Gallico.

2. Counting sheep when you can't get to sleep is one of the most boring experiences of all time. But there are alternatives. For example, you could try eating bananas and drinking milk. Both contain an ingredient called tryptophan which encourages a feeling of calmness. Or follow what colour therapists say and paint your bedroom blue. It's supposed to soothe highly strung people. Dark blue is especially useful for encouraging sleep. And if you're harassed at work, slap a coat of turquoise on the walls. It's said to reduce stress.

In Just Seventeen.

3. What qualifications do you need to be a driving instructor ?
You must have had a full driving licence for four years without any disqualifications. There's no minimum age but licences are rarely granted to anyone under 23. You have to pass the Department of Transport's very tough written and practical exam. There are schools for instructors but you can teach yourself. You have to be an ace driver, have nerves of steel, patience, tolerance, and general good will. In any teaching a sense of humour is also essential !

In Just Seventeen.

4. The pursuit of social success, in the form of prestige or power or both, is the most important obstacle to happiness in a competitive society. I am not denying that success is an ingredient in happiness to most, a very important ingredient. But it does not, by itself, suffice to satisfy most people. You may be rich and admired, but if you have no friends, no interests, no spontaneous useless pleasures, you will be miserable.

Bertrand Russell.

5. "Always remember," said my father, whom I looked upon as the authority on absolutely everything, "that it is vitally important in life to know when to depart. [...] Never stay too long at a party. Better be the first to go. One of the worst things you can do is to stay longer than you are welcome."

Pamela Street.

6. Most of the blame for spoiled holidays can be laid on those too beautiful travel brochures. Nobody in their right mind believes a washingpowder advertisement, but for some reason everyone expects a travel brochure to tell the truth.

C. Ward.

4 **C** Vous trouverez ci-après le compte rendu critique d'un roman, *The Catcher in the Rye*, de J. D. Salinger.

Soulignez les expressions qui organisent le compte rendu.
Réutilisez-les pour rédiger en anglais le compte rendu critique d'un livre que vous connaissez bien.

Here is a novel about a 16-year-old boy who is emotional without being sentimental, dramatic without being melodramatic and honest without being simply obscene. The language has the authentic sound of a boy's voice without being childish or seeming to be written down to that age level. Nor is it merely one more account of adolescence, complete with the usual meditations on youth. The effort has been to make the text, told by the boy himself, as accurate and yet as imaginative as possible. In this, it largely succeeds.

The narrative begins in a boys' prep school in Pennsylvania where the narrator, Holden Caulfield, is seeing one of his teachers for the last time, after having been informed that he is being expelled for failing almost all his courses.

After various incidents with other students, with none of whom he is able to make any close or congenial relationship, he suddenly packs his bags and takes a night train to New York. On the way he meets the mother of one of the boys he knows at school and tells her a fantastic story about her son. He says "I'm the most terrific liar you ever saw in your life", and all the book is a proof of the need he felt for burying his real responses and motivations under a protection of lies, in fear of revealing his essential self.

The balance of the novel deals with his adventures in New York while hiding out from his family and friends.

Various efforts to establish communication with other people fail, and he sneaks home to talk to his younger sister while his parents are out. He decides to run away and Phoebe, the sister, decides to go with him. It is her decision which ties him down and keeps him home, so he does, in the end, find a human warmth.

The book ends with Holden in a mental institution for which the earlier events have hardly prepared the reader. But the story is an engaging and believable one for the most part, full of right observations and sharp insight, and a wonderful sort of grasp of how a boy can create his own world of fantasy and life form.

Chicago Sunday Tribune Magazine of Books.

Employer les mots de liaison

1 C Complétez ces paragraphes en choisissant les mots de liaison appropriés.

1. Indira (Gandhi) was loved (1) not spoilt. (2) she was gawky and long-nosed, some of her relations called her an ugly duckling. Often left on her own, she learnt to take her own decisions. She was intense (3) had a searching, questioning mind. (4) above all she wanted to be worthy of her parents, (5) to help and protect them. She was proud that their pictures, along with pictures of Mahatma Gandhi were found in hundreds of thousands of homes.
(6) Indira was twelve years old, her father became President of the Indian National Congress. At its 1929 session, the Congress had declared that it wanted nothing less than complete independence. (7) she was still very young, Indira was one of those who took the pledge of independence which declared : *The British Government in India has not only deprived the Indian people of their freedom* (8) *has based itself on the exploitation of the masses, and has ruined India economically, politically, culturally* and *spiritually. We believe* (9) *that India must sever the British Connection.*
(10) told that she had to be eighteen to become a member of the Congress Party, Indira decided to form her own organisation. She gathered together a large number of boys and girls and launched the Vanar Sena or "Monkey Brigade". Its members helped the freedom movement by sewing Congress Party flags, cooking food for people (11) took part in demonstrations, giving first aid to workers injured in police conflicts and so on.

1. or - then - but   2. yet - because - although   3. and - for - nevertheless   4. whereas - that's why - but   5. yet - and - while   6. when - since - as   7. because - though - for   8. but - then - yet   9. therefore - although - nevertheless   10. then - also - when   11. whom - which - who

2. *Street Art*
The city street has become a giant arts' laboratory. It would seem that (1) an artist needs a new idea he simply takes a walk in a busy urban street. (2) this is not entirely true, (3) the relationship between the street and commercialization works both ways. Established designers and artists seek inspiration in the street, (4) some of the more fortunate street artists succeed in becoming "established" artists. (5) the media play an important role, acting as a scout for the python-like, all devouring world of business. The media, in their constant search for new stories, can build up any street phenomenon (6) it immediately becomes a household word.

1. since - when - as a consequence. 2. yet - as - for 3. if - while - for 4. because - but - also 5. therefore - unless - here 6. so that - when - although.

3. Charles Dickens, *The Signalman*
... he heard a voice thus calling to him, he was standing at the door of his box, with a flag in his hand, furled round its short pole. One would have thought, considering the nature of the ground, ... he could not have doubted from what quarter the voice came ; ... instead of looking up to ... I stood on the top of the steep cutting nearly over his head, he turned himself about ... looked down the Line. There was something remarkable in his manner of doing so, ... I could not have said for my life what. ... I know it was remarkable enough to attract my notice, ... his figure was foreshortened and shadowed, down in the deep trench, and mine was high above him, so steeped in the glow of an angry sunset, ... I had shaded my eyes with my hand ... I saw him at all.

2 Complete the following sentences in any way you like, using the following link words : whereas - meanwhile - because - therefore - instead of - without - otherwise - however - although - unless - until.

◆ *Watch out for the tenses of the verbs !*

1. He roamed through the streets ... .
2. She bought the book ... .
3. She was quite elegant to look at ... .
4. Well, I think you should wait for her in a café ... .
5. I know you can keep a secret ... .
6. My mother will come to see you tomorrow ... .
7. Do you think you'll manage to go ... .
8. I forgot my umbrella at home ... .
9. He's rather old ... .
10. Their country house is big ... .

4 SUJETS DE RÉDACTION

1 I've got Christmas phobia.

> Dear Virginia,
> Am I the only person in the world to dread Christmas ? Just the sight of the Regent Street lights makes me feel inordinately depressed. I usually spend Christmas quietly with my parents and brother. Last year I didn't send cards and went away on my own to Morocco, but still felt exactly the same gloom. Do I have a Christmas phobia ? Should I just grit my teeth this year and try to join in ? I'd love to know if anyone else dreads it, and how they cope.
> Yours sincerely, Rose

This letter was published in the advice column of a magazine. Read it carefully, then write an answer using expressions of suggestion and advice (refer to *Écrire une lettre*, p. 93), or imagine a dialogue on the subject between Rose and one of her friends.

2 A young couple is trying to decide what to do for the holidays. Study the ads on the opposite page and imagine their conversation. What would *you* like to do ? Explain your choice in a paragraph.

EXODUS

Biking · Discovery · Overland · Walking

RING FOR BROCHURE

Africa!

Safaris & Adventure Holidays
· Namibia · Tanzania · Botswana · Zimbabwe ·
· Kenya · Morocco · South Africa · Madagascar ·

GUERBA

WANTED!

- Keen ears to monitor drums in Senegal
- Art lovers to record Venetian bell towers
- Green fingers to study Chinese silk farms
- Caring hands to unearth Andean Chiefdoms

Earthwatch Membership (£25) puts you in touch with where you are needed across the world. No special skills required. From discovery weekends to four week research projects. It's an experience you'll never forget. Just Call

EARTHWATCH
BECAUSE TOMORROW'S WORLD NEEDS YOU TODAY

EARTHWATCH RESEARCH TEAM

CAMPING & MOBILE HOMES
in a wide choice of sites by the sea

A limited number of Especially Low Priced holidays available now

Hurry! ring for our Brochure

MATTHEWS *makes holidays*

FRANCE

CYCLING FOR SOFTIES
IN FRANCE

9 superb regions from the Loire to Provence.
Delightful hotels.
Delicious food.

24 hour Brochure Hotline

3 The following is a selection of films currently showing in London.
The Antagonists. Based on the novel by Ernest K. Gann the film tells of the Jews' fight for freedom against Caesar's army.
Best Boy. Award-winning documentary by Ira Wohl about a mentally retarded American.
Brothers and Sisters. Thriller set in the north of England about a woman's murder and men's attitudes to women.
The Cat and the Canary. Remake of the comedy thriller about the family of an eccentric millionnaire summoned to hear his will 20 years after his death.
Chariots of Fire. Stirring British film about two athletes, Eric Liddell and Harold Abrahams, striving for excellence in the 1924 Olympics. It says a lot about class, religion and England and is most movingly written by Colin Welland.
Popeye. A busy, jolly, cluttered version of the famous strip-cartoon directed by Robert Altman in holiday humour with Robin William as the squinting hero.

1. Which one would you like to see and why ?
2. Two friends discuss which film they are going to see. Write the dialogue.
3. Describe three films in the same way.

4 You're preparing an article about hitchhiking for a teenagers' magazine.
1. Work out the questionnaire you're going to ask your readers to fill in (ten questions).
2. One of the readers had an anecdote to tell you about his/her experience of hitchhiking : write his/her anecdote in a paragraph of five / ten lines.
3. Write the final article on the subject. (200 words).

5 You're seventy, you look back on your life.
Decide who you are, express your regrets, your wishes, compare your youth and today's world.

6 A page from the diary of an immigrant to the United States (or a discussion between a child and his grandfather /grandmother who was an immigrant).
Say where he comes from, why he left his country, what his hopes are, what difficulties he's faced with.
Speak in the first person.
Use your knowledge of the problem of immigration past and present to make your essay authentic and vivid.

7 Read this article carefully.
Underline the expressions of opinion and all the link-words.
Summarize the article in a few lines.
Make a list of the arguments for and against in a two-column table ; use this table to write a paragraph expressing your own opinion on the issue.

Is signing a contract with your children a solution to family problems ?

"I, Andrew, your dad, want you, Sarah (or Fiona, or Lindsay), my daughter, to know that I love you and you are very precious to me.
I promise that : I will never hit you, or smack you, at any time, ever ;
I think of you as a first-class member of the family and the community ;
I will not shout at you ;
I will always listen to you when you want to speak to me.
My first concern is for your safety and well-being whilst you learn to look out for yourself."
It is a surprisingly simple and straightforward document for something as complicated as rearing a child, but Wray thinks it is an idea all parents should adopt. [...]
Sarah says her friends think the contract is a good idea and wish their own parents would sign one, but the idea of a family contract does not appeal to everyone. Wray has been criticized by some of his friends, and Eileen Orford, a child psychotherapist, says that while she applauds any attempt to be good parents she is unsure about attempting to put the principles of good parenting on paper. "It would be quite dangerous to make a contract which parents could not keep and which doesn't allow them some room for the expression of not altogether nice feelings."
Dr Sebastian Kramer, a consultant psychiatrist at the Tavistock Clinic, is also cautious. "It is a good thing to aim for, but I don't think a contract would be much use for most parents because we wouldn't stick to it," he says. "I sometimes clip my children a bit and don't always answer when they speak to me. I recommend parents try to be good enough, not perfect. I also don't think you should give too much power to children. What they need most of all, because they are intensely conservative, is not to be lied to, and for things to be predictable. Children have the right to be informed, in a way they understand, about what is happening to them."

Times, April 21, 1989.

8 Micro-textes pour l'expression personnelle.

◆ *Comment utiliser ces petits textes ?*

1. *Lisez-les attentivement, cherchez le vocabulaire inconnu dans un dictionnaire.*
2. *Réagissez de manière personnelle en exprimant votre accord ou votre désaccord avec les affirmations qu'ils contiennent. Développez votre position, donnez des exemples.*
3. *N'oubliez pas de construire votre argumentation : faites une introduction et une conclusion.*
4. *Vous aurez sans doute besoin de fonctions de communication telles que l'expression de l'opinion, de l'accord et du désaccord, de la comparaison, etc.*
5. *N'oubliez pas les mots de liaison !*

1. Saving the spotted cats.
As a result of a vigorous campaign, backed by famous people including movie stars and fashion leaders, the International Fur Trade Federation called on its members to stop trading in the skins of Tiger, Snow Leopard and Clouded Leopard. Fashion magazines agreed not to advertise the furs of endangered animals.   *Greenpeace.*

2. Why do people go to see war films ?
There are probably as many reasons as there are people – their favourite star is in it, they were in a war and feel vaguely nostalgic, they like action or they just want to see a film.   *Films & Filming.*

3. Motherhood bars woman from job.
A restaurant owner who refused to employ a waitress because she has four children admitted yesterday : "If a person has full-time responsibility for a number of small children, then it's my experience that they are unreliable."   *The Sun.*

4. Animals should be used for scientific tests and experiments only when there is no practical alternative, and strict statutory control should be imposed over any procedure which causes more than trivial pain.   *Times.*

5. Television will revolutionize politics even beyond what it has to date. [...] Selection of candidates, scheduling of speeches, types of appeal for votes and methods of financing will all have to conform to what television demands. The danger of a demagoguery will be greater than before.   *J. Michener.*

6. ... I do wonder whether there will come a time when we can no longer afford our **wastefulness** – in the rivers, metal wastes everywhere, and atomic wastes and chemical wastes, buried deep in the earth or sunk in the sea. When an Indian village became too deep in its own filth, the inhabitants moved. And we have no place to which to move.   J. Steinbeck.

7. Anyone who has seen or read of the effects of a single **atomic bomb** on Hiroshima in 1945 will realise that thermonuclear weapons equivalent to perhaps a thousand Hiroshimas will cause indescribable damage to this country. The result will be unimaginable death and destruction from which it will take many generations, if ever, to recover. Yet every day we seem to move nearer to the brink.   Letter to the *Times*.

8. Boredom, not long ago the universal complaint of adolescents, is reaching down to younger and younger age groups. It isn't the sort of boredom that children have always known, the endless half-hour before dinner is ready, the tedium of a hot enervating afternoon in the school holidays. What many working class children express now is a self-conscious dissatisfaction with childhood itself, an unquiet impatience to leave it as quickly as possible.
It sometimes seems as though they feel childhood is a conspiracy of adults, forced upon them to keep them from the privileges of being grown up – fashion, money, enjoyment, sex.   Jeremy Seabrook.

9. At the international level sport is frankly mimic warfare. But the significant thing is not the behaviour of the players but the attitude of the spectators : and, behind the spectators, of the nations who work themselves into furies over these absurd contests, and seriously believe – at any rate for short periods – that running, jumping and kicking a ball are tests of national virtue.   George Orwell.

10. Advertising, a sociologist said, must destroy class barriers, for its social effect is to make people dissatisfied with their standard of living, to make them want more consumer goods and services, and particularly to want those previously enjoyed by the socially privileged minorities. The most avid readers of advertisements are people who are either moving up socially or who have bought something that they feel gives them a new status.
  Robert Miller.

RELIRE SON DEVOIR

◆ *Les exercices suivants sont destinés à vous aider à prendre l'habitude de relire votre devoir. Ils vous aideront à éviter des erreurs fréquentes et à concentrer votre attention sur le détail de la forme.*

1 Ce premier exercice vous propose des extraits de devoirs d'élèves. En marge sont signalées les erreurs selon leur nature.
(V = vocabulaire / C = erreur de construction / G = erreur de grammaire).

G	I am not agree with this sentence
G	because I think there are lots of differents aims
G	in the life.
V	This text talks about the American way of life.
G	The narrator uses two differents names to refer to the same person.
V	It's quiet logical.
G	When we will be older we will regret what we did.
C	We can understand more easily things.
V.V.	It's a great quality to arrive to take decisions.
G/G	If I would have to chose between living
G/G	in USA and the Great Britain,
G	I would choose USA.
C	More you think of it and more you will be unhappy.
V	At the difference of the main character, I think
G	one is always responsible of one's actions.
V	He learnt his sister to swim.
G+V	We are many to think that this is the best solution.
G	It exists big differences between these two countries.
V	In first we must try
C	to not make
G	the same mistakes than our parents.

2 Nous vous présentons ici le devoir authentique d'un élève. Il s'agit d'une production faite en temps limité.

Il ne comporte pas de très graves erreurs au plan grammatical. Cependant, la formulation est parfois maladroite.

Dans un premier temps, lisez cette production écrite en essayant de reformuler ce qui a été porté en gras.

Prenez connaissance ensuite de la reformulation.

Sujet : Is having a job considered the normal thing for a woman nowadays ?

PRODUCTION DE L'ÉLÈVE

Women's life has changed a lot in our century : they have claimed the right to be equal to men. So, they can vote *in the same way as* men. But they have also claimed the right to have jobs, whereas they *had* always stayed at home to look after their children, and to clean up their houses. Nowadays, the fact that women *are working* is considered as a normal thing by everyone. But is it *so* simple ? Have men accepted women as *full-times* workers ? Or do they still consider them unconsciously as inferior on the *work* market ?

Today women have fitted into the active life. In fact, *there are* fewer and fewer women *who* stay at home, and more and more *who* work. We can notice that they have reached other areas, like politics.

However, women aren't accepted everywhere and *everytime* yet. Actually, some jobs like lorry *drivers* seem to be reserved to men, since *the concerned areas* are often *male chauvinist*. There are also problems when women *reach high grades* in firms, because unconsciously man is still considered as the authority in our society.

Lastly, in spite of the fact that working mothers *isn't a rare phenomenon*, chores aren't always *divided up* between the *family's members*, and the mother has to *do a double job*.

Despite all these things, women *become* more and more integrated in the working world. In fact, in 1992, in England, male unemployment was 14.2% whereas only 5.8% of "active" women were unemployed.

Finally, *women's job* is considered little by little as a normal thing, but it's very difficult for our society to admit it, because it upsets a lot of habits, and maybe a way of thinking which *had* been accepted for a long time.

COMMENTAIRE / PROPOSITION DE REFORMULATION

- *Women's life* : on pourrait penser qu'il s'agit d'un génitif générique type women's magazine (= a magazine for women). Mieux : **the life** ou **the condition of women**.
- *In the same way as...* : attire trop l'attention sur la manière de : **like** préférable.
- *Had always stayed...* : abus fréquent du past perfect. Il n'existe pas ici de point d'ancrage dans le passé (prétérit) qui permettrait d'employer ce temps. Contraste avec le présent → prétérit : **they stayed**. On pourrait accentuer le contraste en employant **formerly/years ago...**
- *are working ...* : la forme progressive n'est pas justifiée. Il s'agit de la simple constatation d'un fait présent : **work**.
- *so simple* : calqué sur le français "si facile". Il s'agit en fait de la reprise de l'idée précédente et non d'une simple exclamation → **is it that simple ?**
- *Full times* : pourquoi ce "s" à un groupe de mots assimilable à un adjectif ? **full-time**.
- *the work market* : il s'agit de trouver du travail dans le sens d'emploi → **the job market**.
- *there are ... who* : calqué sur le français "il y a ...". La constatation d'un fait présent se fait par l'emploi du présent simple en anglais : **fewer and fewer women stay at home**.
- *everytime* : mot inventé (every time → à chaque fois que ...) : **always** à insérer après aren't ; enlever **and**.
- *lorry drivers* : fait référence aux hommes et non à leur emploi : **lorry driving**.
- *the concerned areas* : concerned maladroit car du domaine de la psychologie (I feel concerned...) ne peut s'appliquer à areas : **such jobs** ...
- *male chauvinist* : s'applique à une personne : **such jobs are male preserves**.
- *reach high grades* : grade = domaine surtout universitaire : **climb the corporate ladder** ou **move into a position of responsibility**.
- *isn't a rare phenomenon* : on ne peut guère appliquer le terme de phenomenon à women ! **working mothers are numerous**.
- *divided up* : il ne s'agit pas de division mais de partage : **shared**.
- *family's members* : abus du génitif : **members of the family**.
- *do a double job* : do incompatible avec job : dans ce sens **work two jobs**.
- *become* : le locuteur attire l'attention sur l'intégration **are becoming** (= despite these things, I can tell you... → emploi de la forme progressive). On peut aussi envisager qu'il s'agit d'un bilan → **have become** serait possible.
- *women's job* : ce n'est pas le travail en lui-même qui est normal mais le fait que les femmes aient un métier → **having a job**.
- *had been accepted* : voir plus haut abus du past perfect : **was accepted**.

3 Q.C.M.

Notes are included ...... the students.
   a. for helping   b. for help   c. for to help   d. to help

I'm sure he ...... agree with you.
   a. will not   b. must be   c. is not   d. has not

This book is most ...... : read it !
   a. interesting   b. interested   c. intresting   d. interessant

I have not seen ...... yet.
   a. somebody   b. anybody   c. nobody   d. no one

I want to be ...... air hostess.
   a. a   b. Ø   c. an   d. no

I have been here ...... two hours.
   a. since   b. for   c. while   d. at

These people ...... very open-minded.
   a. are   b. looks   c. must   d. is

You'll get used ...... it !
   a. done   b. doing   c. to do   d. to doing

She's wearing the same shoes ...... me.
   a. like   b. as   c. than   d. that

He was in a hurry : he ...... early.
   a. leave   b. lived   c. live   d. left

I met her when I was ...... holiday.
   a. the   b. at   c. on   d. in

...... were lots of people.
   a. there   b. these   c. they   d. their

She's very ...... everybody likes her.
   a. fond   b. sympathic   c. nice   d. sympathetic

He works very ....
   a. fastly   b. hard   c. hardly   d. few

...... I think this passage is taken from a novel.
   a. Ø   b. so far as I am concerned   c. me   d. at my opinion.

Queen Victoria ...... in 1901.
   a. has been dead   b. died   c. is dead   d. has died

4 Look at the following groups of sentences, then make up your own sentences showing you know the correct use of the words in italics.

1. *I spoke* to them but they didn't know a word of English.
2. She *told* him once that she had quite made up her mind to refuse the offer.
3. "After all, England's a foreign land to me," he *told* her.
4. "I was pretty bad last night, wasn't I ?" *said* he.
5. "I asked her what she wanted and she *said* something, but I couldn't understand."
6. "*Tell* him to come in, Mary Jane, and close the door."
7. He was astonished to hear that the monks never *spoke*.
8. The others, taken back by this rude speech, could find nothing to *say*.
9. She was leaning on the banisters *listening to* something. Gabriel was surprised at her stillness and strained his ear *to listen* also. But he *could hear* little save the noise of laughter and dispute on the front steps.
10. I remember *hearing* Caruso when he came to this country.
11. The piano was playing a waltz tune and he could *hear* the skirts sweeping against the drawing-room door.

12. He's *dead*, he died when he was only seventeen. Isn't it a terrible thing to *die* so young as that ?
13. I implored of him to go home at once and told him he would get *his death* in the rain. He said he didn't want to *live*.
14. He was so comfortable he didn't want to *leave*.

15. What about the song ? Why does it make you cry ? *It reminds me of* a person long ago who used to sing that song.
16. He *remembered* how the child had smiled at him when he had rescued his little dog from the river.

5 Make sentences to show you know the difference between the following words.

| sensible | big | borrow | economic | to win |
| sensitive | great | lend | economical | to earn |

| between | last | actually | phrase | sympathetic |
| among | least | at present | sentence | pleasant |

DEVOIRS D'UNE HEURE

DEVOIR N° 1 :
I am 22 ... . *134*

DEVOIR N° 2 :
Margaret Drabble, The Middle Ground *135*

DEVOIR N° 3 :
Elia Kazan, The Arrangement *136*

DEVOIR N° 4 :
Margaret Atwood, The Edible Woman *138*

DEVOIR N° 5 :
Little Star, Going Back *139*

DEVOIR N° 6 :
Alan Sillitoe, I was taught to read and write *141*

DEVOIR N° 1

Read this passage from an advice column in a magazine.

I am 22...

I am 22 and <u>have been</u> abroad for my job for nearly six months and really enjoyed it. But when I went home for Christmas, my girlfriend <u>told</u> me it was all over as she'd fallen in love with someone else. It came to me as a great shock. <u>We'd been</u> together for over two years and I can't seem to get her out of my mind.

1 Justify the tenses of the underlined verbs.

2 Write sentences expressing the same ideas, using the following starters.
1. I have been abroad for nearly six months.
It is ......
2. My girlfriend told me it was all over as she'd fallen in love with someone else.
My girlfriend said : "..."
3. I can't seem to get her out of my mind.
I find ... / It is ... (two sentences).

3 Can you imagine what the young man could reproach his former girlfriend with ? Write three sentences in direct speech.

4 Write the answer to his letter as it would be published in the magazine.
Use expressions of advice, "to suggest", parallel increase, for, since or ago.

5 Translate into English.
1. Cette chanson me rappelle les bons moments que nous avons passés ensemble.
2. J'aimerais qu'elle me renvoie les lettres que je lui ai écrites.
3. Je me demande depuis combien de temps elle connaît son nouvel ami.

DEVOIR N° 2

Read this extract carefully.

It was Saturday morning, and she was setting off, as usual, to do the week-end shopping. A few yards down the road she met a girl with a dog. The girl was in tears, standing there crying, leaning on the lamp-post. The girl had red hair, the dog too was golden, a golden retriever.
5 Kate, being tender-hearted, stopped and asked if she could help in any way. The girl, sobbing noisily, poured forth some garbled story of being on the way to meet her father for lunch in town, but her father hated her and hated the dog, she couldn't take the dog into town, she was going to have to abandon him or her father. But surely, Kate argued, the
10 father could not prevent her from taking the dog. The girl [...] continued to cry, then looked at Kate and held out the dog's lead and said, "You have him." "Oh, I can't," said Kate, "I don't want a dog, my house is too small, I have cats, I haven't time for a dog." But the girl could tell she had met a friend, and pressed the lead on Kate. "I'll come back,"
15 she said. "I'll come back for him this afternoon."

Margaret Drabble, The Middle Ground.

1 Justify the use of the underlined articles in English.

2 Turn the passage from *Kate, being tender-hearted...* to *You have him* into a dialogue in direct speech. Make the necessary adjustments so as to be consistent with the elements provided by the text.

3 *"You have him"*, said the girl : express the same idea in three different ways consistent with the meaning of the text.

4 Imagine Kate's thoughts on the way home with the dog (80/100 words). Use exclamatives, expressions of contrast, the present perfect, superlatives...

DEVOIR N° 3

The photograph

In my father's room, there was a small tray with some medicine on it and nothing else. It was a neat room, no sign of human disorder. Where had he lived his life ? Where were the traces of the things he *had* valued ?

Then I saw the photograph.

It was a poor example of that art, in colouring dun[1], in delineation soft. But it was the only picture on his walls. None of his sons, no picture of his wife. There were no photographs of his store, of his stocks, of the National City Bank, or his collection of Oriental Rugs and Carpets. Or of his card-playing cronies[2]. None of them, none of us, meant that much to him. But this photograph did.

The subject was Mount Aergius, the great symmetrical snow-capped mountain which stands over my father's town in Anatolia, the place of his birth. Aergius, the lofty, clean, perfect mountain. Here it was, now, the magnet of whatever longing my father still had aching within him, the one image of love on the old man's wall.

The mountain represented in that photograph seemed to be demanding some judgment of me, some verdict. What do you think, it seemed to say, what do you really think ? And if I had been forced to answer and give a verdict at that moment, I would have had to say that I thought the whole passage of my family to this country had been a failure, not the country's fault perhaps, but the inevitable result of the time and the spirit in the air in those days. The symbols of affluence gained had been empty even by the standards of the market place. The money they had acquired wasn't worth much ; they had found that out in 1929. As for the other acquisitions - the homes, the furniture, the cars, the pianos, the clothes, the land - they had meant nothing. These men who had cried America, America ! as the century died had come here looking for freedom and the other human things, and all they had found for themselves was the freedom to make as much money as possible.

Why had my family left such a beautiful place ? There were reasons, true, but the question must have remained in my father's heart : what had he acquired here to make that migration worthwhile ? He must have wondered. Or else the photograph could not have been the only thing on his wall.

35 Something that picture made him feel would not rest and die. They had left that country with its running water, and its orchards of fruit, and all, all that my grandmother never stopped talking about ; they had left that to find a better place to live, and all they had found was a better place to make money.

Elia Kazan, The Arrangement.

1. dun = dull greyish-brown
2. cronies = chums, friends

1 What does this passage tell us about the character of the hero's father ? What did Mount Aergius represent for him ?

2 What were his expectations when he came to America ? Were they fulfilled ? Explain the contradiction in the following lines : *They had left that to find a better place to live, and all they had found was a better place to make money...* (l. 37-38).

3 Justify the use of italics in line 4 ("he *had* valued").

4 *The mountain ... seemed **to be demanding**...* (l. 17). Why does the narrator use the verbal form "be demanding" and not "demand" ?

5 Analyse the use of "had + past participle" in the following sentences.
*if I **had been forced** to answer...* (l. 19) : ...
*the whole passage of my family to this country **had been** a failure...* (l. 21) : ...
*they **had found** that out in 1929...* (l. 25) : ...

6 What shades of meaning do the modals bring in the following sentences (refer to the last paragraph).
*he **must** have wondered...* (l. 33) : ...
*the photograph **could** not have been the only thing on his wall...* (l. 34) : ...
*Something ... **would** not rest...* (l. 35) : ...

7 Translate from *Then I saw the photograph...* (l. 5) to *the old man's wall* (l. 16).

DEVOIR N° 4

Marian was walking slowly down the aisle, keeping pace with the gentle music that swelled and rippled around her. "Beans," she said. She found the kind marked "Vegetarian" and tossed two cans into her wire cart.
The music swung into a tinkly waltz ; she proceeded down the aisle, trying to concentrate on her list. She resented the music because she knew why it was there : it was supposed to lull you into a euphoric trance, lower your sales resistance to the point at which all things are desirable. Every time she walked into the supermarket and heard the lilting sounds coming from the concealed loudspeakers she remembered an article she had read about cows who gave more milk when sweet music was played to them. But because she knew what they were up to didn't mean she was immune. These days, if she wasn't careful, she found herself pushing the cart like a somnambulist, eyes fixed, swaying slightly, her hands twitching with the impulse to reach out and grab anything with a bright label. She had begun to defend herself with lists, which she printed in block letters before setting out, willing herself to buy nothing, however deceptively-priced or subliminally-packaged, except what was written there. When she was feeling unusually susceptible she would tick the things off the list with a pencil as an additional counter-charm.
But in some ways they would always be successful : they couldn't miss. You had to buy something sometime. She knew enough about it from the office to realize that the choice between, for instance, two brands of soap or two cans of tomato juice was not what could be called a rational one. In the products, the things themselves, there was no real difference. How did you choose then ? You could only abandon yourself to the soothing music and make a random snatch. You let the thing in you that was supposed to respond to the labels just respond, whatever it was... [...]
"Noodles," she said. She glanced up from her list just in time to avoid collision with a plump lady in frazzled muskrat. "Oh no, they've put another brand on the market." She knew the noodle business : several of her afternoons had been spent in stores in the Italian section, counting the endless varieties and brands of *pasta*. She glared at the noodles, stacks of them, identical in their cellopacks, then shut her eyes, shot out her hand and closed her fingers on a package. Any package.

Margaret Atwood, *The Edible Woman*.

1 C Translate from line 1 to line 11 (*music was played to them*).

2 C Study the writer's judgment on the consumer society through her account of Marian's experience at the supermarket.

DEVOIR N° 5

Going Back

These past few years, it's been a very "in" thing to talk about how you're going back to the reservation when you finish school. Many will go, but few will stay. They'll return to the city in two or three years, disillusioned. It is easy to talk about Indian unity, Indian power, the strength of the land, Indian input, but it's hard to put these ideas to work on a reservation where the main thing people want is something to eat.

The first thing that hits you when you go home – after you realize that you *live* there now, and you're not leaving in a few weeks – is that your college degrees don't give you the prestige on the reservation that you assumed they would ; BIA[1] people and some councilmen may be impressed, your own family may be proud, but people couldn't care less. You've been away for a long time and they study you for a while.

Some try to prove themselves one of the people by drinking around a lot, saying see I'm still one of you but the people trying to make up their mind about you wonder because we don't need more drunken Indians on the reservation, we have enough. Some miss their group at school, heads especially try to set up a copy of this little group on the reservation. They find they have to include whites, young VISTAs[2] or public health people, there not being enough heads around the reservation that are past high school age. And the people hear rumours. Some go into a frenzy of activity to prove themselves, they get involved in everything, but still miss the point because they don't really care about the people – they care American style about getting the job done. [...] You find yourself being as paternal as the BIA superintendent and maybe more patronizing. It's hard to realize that these people are the ones you've spoken of for so long as "my people". When you finally realize that they don't belong to you but that you belong to your tribe then you're really on your way back. Then you can find what your spot is in the circle of your tribal world. And just maybe you'll be an Indian again.

Little Star *(Tribe unknown), 1970,*
from Peter Nabokov, *Native American Testimony.*

1. the BIA = the Bureau of Indian Affairs
2. VISTAs = social workers

COMPRÉHENSION

1 C Explain *it's been a very "in" thing.*

2 C *"Many will go, but few will stay."* Where ?

3 C What ideas are hard to put to work on an Indian reservation ? Why ?

4 C Cite three examples of what some Native Americans returning to their reservations do to try and fit back into the life of their people. Why does each attempt prove to be a failure ?

Attempt	Reasons for the failure
......	......
......	......
......	......

5 C According to Little Star, when can an Indian really reenter the tribal community ?

COMPÉTENCE LINGUISTIQUE

1 C Time or tense ? Analyse the following verbal forms.
many **will go** (l. 2) : ...
you'**re not leaving** (l. 8) : ...
they **would** (l. 10) : ...

2 C Mettez au singulier le segment en gras de la phrase.
*They find they have to include **whites, young VISTAs or public health people**.*

3 C Turn into indirect speech using an introductory verb in the past. Do not use the verbs to say or to tell.
You miss the exciting discussions about what it means to be an Indian.
Educated Indians have always had a difficult time working on their own reservations.
They'll return to the city in two or three years, disillusioned.

DEVOIR N° 6

I was taught to read and write at school, but not much else. The teachers pushed me to the back, and ignored me. But out of spite, and perhaps a desire to please, I got good marks in reading and writing. Then they kept me at the back of the class because I didn't seem to need the same atten-
5 tion as those duffers[1] who couldn't even learn that much. At about this time, when I was seven, my mother and grandmother got wind of a nearby house that had been abandoned. Someone had done a moonlight flit to Birmingham and left a lot of stuff behind because the van was full. So my mother shuf-
fled herself through the scullery window one afternoon and opened the
10 door for me and Grandma. There wasn't much loot except a few old tats and pots, but I went into the parlour and saw that the floor was covered with large books of music. They were scattered everywhere and I sat looking through them, fascinated by the sheets of complex musical notation. They stood out black and plain – quavers[2] and crotchets[3] and minims[4],
15 words I already knew from school – and I ran my fingers over them as if they were written in braille. I took two away under my arm, and was proud to own them, though later they disappeared to I don't know where, but for years afterwards those lines of soundless music went through my dreams.

Alan Sillitoe.

1. *duffers* : cancres
2. *quavers* : croches
3. *crotchets* : blanches
4. *minims* : noires

1 Rephrase the following sentences using the given prompts.
The teachers pushed me to the back. (l. 1-2)
I ...

But out of spite... writing. (l. 2-3)
I got good marks because...

Someone had left a lot of stuff behind. (l. 7-8)
A lot of stuff...

2 Ask the question corresponding to the words in heavy type.
Someone had left a lot of stuff behind. (l. 7-8)
The floor was covered with **large books of music**. (l. 11-12)
I took **two away**. (l. 16)
They disappeared to **I don't know where**. (l. 17)
For years those lines of soundless music went through my dreams. (l. 18)
For years **those lines of soundless music** went through my dreams. (l. 18)

3 Translate from line 1 (*I was taught*) to line 7 (*abandoned*).

EXAMENS BLANCS

SUJET 1, SÉRIES L, ES, S (LV1)
Amy Tan, The Joy Luck Club *144*

SUJET 2, SÉRIES L, ES, S (LV1)
Kazuo Ishiguro, The Remains of the Day *148*

SUJET 3, SÉRIES TECHNOLOGIQUES (LV1)
Patricia Highsmith, A Suspension of Mercy *152*

SUJET 4, SÉRIE L (LV2)
Alison Lurie, The War between the Tates *155*

Examen blanc

Sujet 1, Séries L, ES, S (LV 1)

On a cold spring afternoon, while walking home from school, I detoured through the playground at the end of our alley. I saw a group of old men, two seated across a folding table playing a game of chess, others smoking pipes, eating peanuts, and watching. I ran home and grabbed Vincent's chess set, which was bound in a cardboard box with rubber bands. I also carefully selected two prized rolls of Life Savers. I came back to the park and approached a man who was observing the game.
"Want to play ?" I asked him. His face widened with surprise and he grinned as he looked at the box under my arm.
"Little sister, been a long time since I play with dolls," he said, smiling benevolently. I quickly put the box down next to him on the bench and displayed my retort.
Lau Po, as he allowed me to call him, turned out to be a much better player than my brothers. I lost many games and many Life Savers. But over the weeks, with each diminishing roll of candies, I added new secrets. [...] By the end of the summer, Lau Po had taught me all he knew, and I had become a better chess player.
A small weekend crowd of Chinese people and tourists would gather as I played and defeated my opponents one by one. My mother would join the crowds during these outdoor exhibition games. She sat proudly on the bench, telling my admirers with proper Chinese humility, "Is luck."
A man who watched me play in the park suggested that my mother allow me to play in local chess tournaments. My mother smiled graciously, an answer that meant nothing. I desperately wanted to go, but I bit back my tongue. I knew she would not let me play among strangers. So as we walked home I said in a small voice that I didn't want to play in the local tournament. They would have American rules. If I lost I would bring shame on my family.
"Is shame you fall down nobody push you," said my mother.
During my first tournament, my mother sat with me in the front row as I waited for my turn. I frequently bounced my legs to unstick them from the cold metal seat of the folding chair. When my name was called my mother unwrapped something in her lap. It was her *chang*, a small tablet of red jade which held the sun's fire. "Is luck," she whispered, and tucked it into my dress pocket. I turned to my opponent, a fifteen-year-old boy from Oakland. He looked at me wrinkling his nose.

As I began to play, the boy disappeared, the color ran out of the room, and I saw only my white pieces and his black ones waiting on the other side. A light wind began blowing past my ears. It whispered secrets only I could hear.

"Blow from the South," it murmured. "The wind leaves no trail." I saw a clear path, the traps to avoid. The crowd rustled. "Shhh ! Shhh !" said the corners of the room. The wind blew stronger. "Throw sand from the East to distract him." The knight came forward ready for sacrifice. The wind hissed, louder and louder. "Blow, blow, blow. He cannot see. He is blind now. Make him lean away from the wind so he is easier to knock down."

"Check," I said as the wind roared with laughter. The wind died down to little puffs, my own breath.

My mother placed my first trophy next to a plastic chess set that the neighborhood Tao society had given to me. As she wiped each piece with a soft cloth, she said, "Next time win more, lose less."

"Ma, it's not how many pieces you lose," I said. "Sometimes you need to lose pieces to get ahead."

"Better to lose less, see if you really need."

At the next tournament, I won again, but it was my mother who wore the triumphant grin.

"Lost eight piece this time. Last time was eleven. What I tell you ? Better off lose less !" I was annoyed, but I couldn't say anything.

Amy Tan, *The Joy Luck Club*.

COMPRÉHENSION

Partie commune aux trois séries

1 C Pick out the information about the narrator's age, sex and origin (quote from the text).

2 C What details reveal the narrator is really gifted at chess ?

3 C *Is shame you fall down nobody push you.* (l. 29)
Can you :
a. express the same idea in correct English ?
b. explain its meaning in the context ?

4 C a. Put the following sentences into the right chronological order.
1. She attracted a lot of attention.
2. Her first opponent in the local tournament was a fifteen-year-old boy.
3. Lau Po taught her all he knew within a few months.

4. She played her first competitions in the park next to her home.
5. She was so deep in concentration that she forgot everything around her.
6. The narrator joined a group of old men playing chess.
7. Her mother had her own views on chess playing.
8. She talked her mother into allowing her to play in local tournaments.
9. Her mother gave her a lucky charm.

❏ ❏ ❏ ❏ ❏ ❏ ❏ ❏ ❏

b. Using these elements write a short summary of the text. (80 words)

5 C Which of the following titles would best apply to the text ? Justify.
a. The making of a chess champion.
b. First generation American.
c. Mother and child.

Série L uniquement

6 C What does the use of **would** (l. 18 and 19) show ?

7 C A number of sentences in this text are not correct English : list them. What grammatical category do they fall into ? Justify their use by the author.

8 C What does this text reveal about the relationship between the narrator and her mother ? (120 words)

9 Further in the novel we can read : "They ran a photo of me [the narrator] in *Life Magazine* next to a quote in which Bobby Fischer[1] said, 'There will never be a woman grand master'."
Do you agree that women can never equal men in some fields ? Give examples to justify your opinion. (200 words).

10 C Translate into French from *As I began to play...* (l. 37) to *my own breath* (l. 48).

1. a famous chess grand master.

Compétence linguistique

Séries ES et S uniquement

1 C Express the same idea using the following starters.

1. A man [...] suggested that my mother allow me to play in local chess tournaments.
You ...
What ... ?

2. If I lost I would bring shame on my family.
If I lose ...
If I had lost ...

3. "been a long time since I play with dolls."
It's ...
I haven't ...

2 C Turn the passage from l. 22 (*A man ...*) to l. 28 (*on my family*) into the present.

3 C Translate from *A small weekend crowd...* (l. 18) to *Is luck* (l. 21).

Expression

Séries ES et S uniquement

Vous traiterez l'un des deux sujets au choix (de 300 à 350 mots).

1 What qualities are required to become a great champion or artist ? Would *you* be ready to make the necessary sacrifices ?

2 When she played the narrator was so entranced that she forgot everything around her. Have you ever experienced the same feeling ? Describe the circumstances.

Examen blanc

Sujet 2, Séries L, ES, S (LV1)

"I can see you are not very satisfied, Mr Stevens," Miss Kenton said. "Do you not believe me ?" "Oh, it's not that, Mrs Benn, not that at all. It's just that the fact remains, you do not seem to have been happy over the years. That is to say – forgive me – you have taken it on yourself
5   to leave your husband on a number of occasions. If he does not mistreat you, then, well … one is rather mystified as to the cause of your unhappiness."
I looked out into the drizzle again. Eventually, I heard Miss Kenton say behind me : "Mr Stevens, how can I explain ? I hardly know myself
10 why I do such things. But it's true, I've left three times now." She paused a moment, during which time I continued to gaze out towards the fields on the other side of the road. Then she said : "I suppose, Mr Stevens, you're asking whether or not I love my husband."
"Really, Mrs Benn, I would hardly presume…"
15 "I feel I should answer you, Mr Stevens. As you say, we may not meet again for many years. Yes, I do love my husband. I didn't at first. I didn't at first for a long time. When I left Darlington Hall all those years ago, I never realized I was really, truly leaving. I believe I thought of it as simply another ruse, Mr Stevens, to annoy you. It was a shock to come
20 out here and find myself married. For a long time, I was very unhappy, very unhappy indeed. But then year after year went by, there was the war, Catherine grew up, and one day I realized I loved my husband. You spend so much time with someone, you find you get used to him. He's a kind, steady man, and yes, Mr Stevens, I've grown to love him."
25 Miss Kenton fell silent again for a moment. Then she went on :
"But that doesn't mean to say, of course, there aren't occasions now and then – extremely desolate occasions when you think to yourself : "What a terrible mistake I've made with my life." And you get to thinking about a different life, a *better* life you might have had. For instance, I get to
30 thinking about a life I might have had with you, Mr Stevens. And I suppose that's when I get angry over some trivial little thing and leave. But each time I do so, I realize before long – my rightful place is with my husband. After all, there's no turning back the clock now. One can't be forever dwelling on what might have been. One should realize one has as
35 good as most, perhaps better, and be grateful."
I do not think I responded immediately, for it took me a moment or two

to fully digest these words of Miss Kenton. Moreover, as you might appreciate, their implications were such as to provoke a certain degree of sorrow within me. Indeed – why should I not admit it ? – at that moment, my heart was breaking. Before long, however, I turned to her and said with a smile :
"You're very correct, Mrs Benn. As you say, it is too late to turn back the clock. Indeed, I would not be able to rest if I thought such ideas were the cause of unhappiness for you and your husband. We must each of us, as you point out, be grateful for what we *do* have. And from what you tell me, Mrs Benn, you have reason to be contented. In fact I would venture, what with Mr Benn retiring and with grandchildren on the way, that you and Mr Benn have some extremely happy years before you. You really mustn't let any more foolish ideas come between yourself and the happiness you deserve."
"Of course, you're right, Mr Stevens. You're so kind." "Ah, Mrs Benn, that appears to be the bus coming now."
I stepped outside and signalled, while Miss Kenton rose and came to the edge of the shelter. Only as the bus pulled up did I glance at Miss Kenton and perceived that her eyes had filled with tears.

Kazuo Ishiguro, *The Remains of the Day*.

COMPRÉHENSION

Partie commune aux trois séries

1 **Justify the following statements with appropriate quotations.**
– Mr Stevens did not fully understand the reason why Miss Kenton had left her husband several times.
– The scene he describes took place on a wet day.
– Miss Kenton's departures from her home were caused by unimportant matters.
– Her attitude was seemingly resigned.
– Although Mr Stevens was very upset by Mrs Benn's words, he did not show it.
– He advised her to stay with her husband and never leave again.
– Mrs Benn wished in fact that things had been different.

2 **Why does the narrator use two different names i.e. Miss Kenton and Mrs Benn when referring to the same person ? (50 words).**

3 Choose adjectives from the following list to describe Mr Stevens's reaction to Miss Kenton's words.

He was amused - indifferent - upset - annoyed - dejected - thrilled - hopeful.

Justify your choice with a quotation.

4 Explain : *there is no turning back the clock* (l. 33). (30 words)

Série L uniquement

5 What shades of meaning do the following modals convey ?
*How **can** I explain ?* (l. 9)
*I feel I **should** answer you...* (l. 15)
*We **may** not meet...* (l. 15)
*You **might** appreciate...* (l. 37)
*You **mustn't** let...* (l. 49)

6 *I get to thinking about a life I might have had...* (l. 29-30)
In what circumstances could somebody say *I get to thinking about a life I might have...* ?

7 What were the *implications* of Miss Kenton's words (refer to l. 38) ? (50 words)

8 Do you agree with Miss Kenton's words : *one can't be forever dwelling on what might have been* ? (200 words)

9 Traduisez de la ligne 16 (*Yes, I do love my husband...*) à la ligne 28 (*... I've made with my life*).

COMPÉTENCE LINGUISTIQUE

Séries ES et S uniquement

1 Rephrase the following sentences using the given prompts.
How can I explain? She wondered ......
I hardly know myself why I do such things. Miss Kenton explained ......
For a long time I was very unhappy. She recognized ......

2 The following passage precedes the passage you have studied. Put the verbs in brackets into the correct tense.

The rain still (*fall*) steadily as we (*get*) out of the car and (*hurry*) towards the shelter. [...] Inside the paint (*peel*) everywhere, but the place (*be*) clean enough. Miss Kenton (*seat*) herself on the bench provided, while I (*remain*) on my feet where I (*can*) command a view on the approaching bus.
After we (*wait*) in silence for a few minutes, I finally (*bring*) myself to say : "Excuse me, Mrs Benn. But the fact is we may not meet again for a long time. I wonder if you would perhaps permit me to ask you something of a rather personal order. It is something that (*trouble*) me for some time."

3 This is the end of the characters' conversation. Fill in the blanks with the appropriate modals.

"Now, Mrs Benn, you .... take good care of yourself. Many say retirement is the best part of life for a married couple. You .... do all you ...... to make these years happy ones for yourself and your husband. We ...... never meet again, Mrs Benn, so I .... ask you to take good heed of what I am saying."
"I ......, Mr Stevens, thank you. And thank you for the lift. It was so very kind of you. It was so nice to see you again."

EXPRESSION

Séries ES et S uniquement

Vous traiterez l'un des deux sujets au choix. (300 mots)

1 *The Remains of the Day* was adapted for the screen in 1993. Do dramatizations ruin the original works ? Discuss the pros and cons.

2 Do you agree with Mr Stevens's statement : *Retirement is the best part of life for a married couple ?*

Examen blanc

Sujet 3, Séries technologiques (LV1)

The next morning at 10, a young police constable knocked on Sydney's door. The young officer was blond, fresh-faced and very earnest behind his smile. He pulled out a notebook and a fountain-pen and Sydney offered him a chair. He sat down stiffly, and prepared to write on his
5 knees. "It's about your wife. Have you heard anything from her ?"
"Not a thing," Sydney said. He sat down on the sofa.
The first questions were of the kind Sydney anticipated. The date he had seen her last ? July 2. Where ? He had put her on the train to London at Ipswich that morning, Saturday, around 11.30 a.m. Where did she
10 say she was going ? She said to her mother's. What kind of mood had she been in ? In quite a good mood. She was going to do some painting, and she wanted to be by herself for a while. Wasn't it unusual that she hadn't written a word to him or to anyone since ? No, not really because she had said she wouldn't write to him until she wanted to come
15 back, and she asked him not to try to communicate with her. But wasn't it unusual that she hadn't written to her mother ? Perhaps it was.
Sydney rubbed his palms together slowly between his knees, and waited attentively for the next questions.
"The police are looking around Brighton now, but it's important that
20 we get some information from you, too. Do you know any other places she might have gone ?"
"I can't think of any."
"Did she say how long she might be away ?"
"Not specifically. She said,' No matter how long I'm gone –' that she
25 didn't want me to try to find her. I gathered it could be months. Maybe six months."
"Really ?" He wrote it down. "She said that ?"
"She said she didn't know. " Sydney shrugged a little, nervously. "She took two suitcases with her and some of her winter clothes. She thought
30 – some time apart might do us both good," Sidney said, feeling himself sliding deeper into suspicious sounding replies, perfectly truthful replies, yet he was doing what murderers always did, say their victims had said they would be absent for an indefinite length of time.
"In that case, maybe there's not so much reason for Mrs Bartleby's
35 parents to be worried," said the constable.
"No, and I suppose something's in the papers this morning. I only saw

The Times. If my wife knows her family's so concerned, she'll communicate. Probably today."

"It's in the papers this morning with a photograph. It's in the *Express*. Mrs Bartleby's parents don't know she might stay away as long as six months?" the young constable asked with a frown.

"I don't know. I didn't tell her mother for fear she might be more worried. Also because I wasn't sure Alicia really would stay away that long."

Patricia Highsmith, *A Suspension of Mercy*.

COMPRÉHENSION

1 Right or wrong ? Circle the right answer. Justify by quoting from the text.

1. Sydney had expected the police constable's visit.
R   W   …
2. His wife has left him for another man.
R   W   …
3. She took very little luggage with her.
R   W   …
4. Sydney was worried because she hadn't been in touch for a long time.
R   W   …
5. The policeman suspected Sydney of lying to him.
R   W   …
6. Sydney realized his answers might sound suspicious.
R   W   …
7. Alicia's parents informed the press that their daughter was missing.
R   W   …
8. The police hadn't started their investigations yet.
R   W   …

2 Worried - serious - determined - attentive - intrigued - uneasy. Which of these adjectives can be applied to :
Sydney : …
The police constable : …
Alicia : …
Her parents : …

3 Quote two sentences from the text explaining why, according to Sydney, Alicia had decided to go away for a while.

4 Translate into French from *The first questions…* (l. 7) to *… quite a good mood.* (l. 11)

EXPRESSION

1 What reasons can the police have to suspect Sydney of having killed his wife ? Use the information provided in the text to justify your answer. (50 words)

2 Sydney writes a letter to his parents-in-law to explain why they shouldn't worry. (100 words)

Examen blanc

Sujet 4, Série L (LV2)

There was a loud knock on the door, repeated impatiently while he was crossing the room to answer it. He opened the door. There in the hall stood Holman Turner, with the light behind him and his face dark. Christ, he's found out, was Will's first thought ; his first impulse was to shut the door again.
"I thought it was about time I came to see you," Holman said in a somewhat strained voice. "Are you busy ?"
"No, no," replied Will, looking to see if his guest were carrying a weapon. PROF SHOOTS (STABS, BASHES ?) WIFE'S BOYFRIEND Holman appeared to be unarmed. "Come on in," Will heard himself say. Holman came in. I am a couple of inches taller, but we are about evenly matched as to weight, Will decided, measuring him in the dim light.
"Convenient place you have here."
"Thank you." Convenient for what ? Maybe he only suspects. He's come to test me. "Like a drink ?" he said as casually as he could manage.
"Thanks, I could use one."
But look how he's staring at me. In that part of the long attic room which constituted his kitchen, Will opened a drawer and took out the bread knife. "Bourbon ?" he asked. The bread knife was not very sharp. Also, it was awkwardly obvious. His Boy Scout knife would have been better, but he had lent it to Henry Oska, a Boy Scout.
"Anything."
One doesn't murder a man from whom one has just accepted a drink, surely. Will replaced the knife. But he felt some reluctance to turn his back to Holman, and he kept looking round while he put in the ice and water.
"Jack Daniels, hm ?" Holman observed.
"Why not." On the other hand, Holman might consider it the Somerset Maugham[1] kind of thing to do, to have a drink with your rival before you killed him. He opened the drawer again.
"Cheers," he said handing Holman his glass and placing the bread knife near by on the coffee-table, together with a loaf of bread which had unfortunately already been sliced by the bakery. They drank in silence. Well, go ahead, you don't expect me to bring the subject, do you ? Will thought.

1. Comme dans un roman de W. Somerset Maugham (1874-1965).

35 "Nice place you have," Holman said again. Will realized that he was slightly drunk.
"Thank you."
"I always wanted a place like this, live alone, lots of things you can do in a place like this." Very slowly Holman began to take something large
40 and metallic out of his pocket. Drunk, he would be more likely to shoot on impulse, though maybe not as accurate. Will leaned forward and put his hand on the hilt of the bread knife.
"Yeah ; you can accomplish a lot when you have a place like this and no responsibilities," Holman said. He took out of his pocket a large
45 heavy cigarette-lighter. "Smoke ?"

Alison Lurie, *The War between the Tates.*

COMPRÉHENSION

1 Right or wrong ? Circle the right answer. Justify by quoting from the text.
1. The whole passage is seen from Holman Turner's point of view. R W ...
2. It's the first time Holman has come to Will's place. R W ...
3. Will considers Holman as a friend. R W ...

2 Pick out three sentences showing that Will
a. fears Holman Turner might suspect that he's having an affair with his wife (3 quotes) ;
1. ...   2. ...   3. ...

b. is afraid he might have come to kill him (3 quotes).
1. ...   2. ...   3. ...

3 Will considers using the bread knife to defend himself, should Holman be armed ; explain the following indications by quoting from the text.

	Why ?
Will opened a drawer and took out the bread knife. (l. 18)	......
Will replaced the knife. (l. 24)	......
Will placed the bread knife near by on the coffee-table. (l. 30)	......
Will [...] put his hand on the hilt of the bread knife. (l. 41)	......

4 **The tone of the text is :**
❏ dramatic ❏ humorous ❏ serious

TRADUCTION

Translate from *I thought it was about time...* (l. 6) **to** *in the dim light* (l. 12).

EXPRESSION

Vous traiterez l'un des deux sujets suivants. (300 mots environ)

1 Have you ever been confronted with an embarrassing situation ? Describe the situation and explain how you managed to get out of it.

2 Holman says : *I always wanted a place like this, lots of things you can do in a place like this.*
Do you think the work place has an influence on the way people work ? Give examples of what could be done to improve the working conditions in offices, factories, schools…

COMPÉTENCE LINGUISTIQUE

1 **Complete the following sentences with the appropriate modal, consistent with the meaning of the text. You may have to use negative forms.**

1. Whoever was knocking so loud on the door … (*be*) angry.
2. Will wondered whether his guest … (*carry*) a weapon.
3. Will … (*lend*) his Boy Scout knife to Henry Oska.
4. One … (*murder*) a man from whom one has just accepted a drink.
5. Holman began to take something large and metallic out of his pocket : it … (*be*) a gun.

2 **Complete with the appropriate question-tag.**

1. Come on in, … ?
2. He's found out, … ?
3. Let's have a drink, … ?
4. You like Bourbon, … ?
5. Lots of things you can do in a place like this, … ?

3 Write sentences using comparatives or superlatives.

1. Holman - Will - tall
   Holman ...
2. Will - Holman - drunk
   Will ...
3. The bread knife - his Boy Scout knife - sharp
   The bread knife ...
4. Jack Daniels - Scotch Whisky - good
   ...
5. A drunk man - a sober man - dangerous
   ...

CORRIGÉS

COMPRÉHENSION

1. COMPRENDRE UN TEXTE COURT

Matching (p. 11-12)
1/g – 2/d – 3/a – 4/e – 5/b – 6/c – 7/f – 8/h

Rétablir la ponctuation (p. 12-13)
1. – "I won't get down, thank you," she said ,"I just came down to tell you that I'm going to be married."
– "What !"
– "Who to ?"
– "Cathy, how grand !"
– "When ?"
– "Tomorrow," said Cathleen quietly.

Trouver le mot manquant (p. 13-14)
2.1. *Newsweek* (p. 14)
Tats = women.
Plusieurs indices peuvent vous amener à cette réponse :
– "the convention", "its diversity of age, income, race, occupation or opinion" vous indique qu'il s'agit d'êtres humains.
– "three presidents' wives", "abortion", "their children", qu'il s'agit de femmes.

Chasser l'intrus (p. 15-16)
1. seasons – reasons / thick – sick / word – world
2. manner – matter / pupils – people
3. lake – lack
4. cereals – serials / deterrent – detergent / read – reach
5. fly – flee / flood – flock
6. Call – Wall / honey – money
7. chancing – changing / piece – peace
8. feeling – falling / petal – metal / sandals – vandals / cave – save
9. relief – belief / probabilities – possibilities
10. Fiend – Friend / mime – time

Trouver des équivalents (p. 18-19)
1. unwillingness = reluctance – to manage successfully = to cope with – to push = to cram – to feel underprivileged = to feel a sense of deprivation

2. to pull out of = to drag – affected by a disaster = stricken – bits of broken stone = rubble - cost = toll – to concentrate = to focus – something that brings comfort = blessing – thick mud = slime – to die from hunger = to starve

3. to make better = to improve – abilities to do something well = skills – to practice = to train – to show clearly = to highlight – to be the right size = to fit – to teach = to coach

4. reason = grounds – in fact = actually – greatest = utmost – excitement = thrill – shocking fact = outrage – to come to one's mind = to occur

Corrigés

2. DE LA COMPRÉHENSION AU RÉSUMÉ

What were they asked? (p. 21-22)
Question 1 : Could you live without TV?
Who? Derek Jameson, Mary White.

Choose the headline (p. 22-23)
1. 1. ROOM FOR SMOKERS
The clues : a total ban was rejected / will continue to be smoke-free areas.
2. VIVISECTION PROTEST
The clues : to protest against the use of animals for scientific experiments.
3. SPACE INVADERS
The clues : a hidden invasion / having their minds probed from afar.

2. WANTED : MAN WITH MISSING EAR (… *among others*)
The actual headline was "Ear today…", an allusion to the saying "Here today, gone tomorrow".

3. FAMOUS PAINTINGS FOUND IN ABANDONED FARM
Two paintings by Degas, stolen from a museum in northern Italy earlier this month, have been recovered. The works were among twenty paintings that went missing from a museum in Ferrara. Police recovered the artwork on Friday in an abandoned farm during a raid in which seven persons were arrested.

L'emploi du passif est caractéristique du style journalistique.

Find the right order (p. 23-25)
2. (*p. 24*)
1. b - a - d - c / 2. a - d - e - c - b / 3. d - b - a - g - f - e - c
Les repères logiques et chronologiques doivent vous orienter, par exemple dans le paragraphe 1 :
- on one side / on the other,
- in recent years / last week,
- planned to sell / it's decided.

3. While you two were at dinner I went to Valerie Hallstrom's place. It's an old brownstone with a basement and three floors. She owns it all and everything inside is very expensive. […] I'll tell you in a moment what I found. Now that little inspection took me from about eight-thirty to nine-thirty. At nine-thirty the telephone rang. **I waited until it had stopped and left, by way of the basement**. I sat in my car on the opposite side of the street and waited. At about ten-thirty a man, carrying a small briefcase, entered the house. **He used a key**. He didn't come out. He didn't switch on any lights. I waited until I saw Valerie Hallstrom come home. I saw you pass by in the limousine. I saw the lights go on in the living room and in the bedroom, but I couldn't see inside because the drapes were drawn. **About ten minutes later the man, still carrying the briefcase, came out**. He walked westward, across the town. **I followed him**. He flagged a taxi and beat the lights at the next intersection, so I lost him. I stopped at a pay phone and called Valerie Hallstrom's number. No one answered it.

True or false? (p. 25-27)

1. 1. *Newsweek* (p. 25-26)
a. Wrong : Recognizing the importance of physical fitness is **hardly a new idea** (l. 1).
b. Right : Automation and high technology have removed physical exercise from countless daily routines (l. 3).
c. Right : The accumulated stresses and pressures of office and home life (l. 5).
d. Wrong : because of the economic recession (l. 7).

2. Maeve Binchy,
Light a Penny Candle (p. 26)
Evacuated from blitz-battered London, genteel Elizabeth White is sent to stay with the boisterous Irish O'Connors. It is the beginning of an unshakeable bond between Elizabeth and Aisling O'Connor which will survive twenty turbulent years. Writing with warmth, wit and great compassion, Maeve Binchy tells a magnificent story of the lives and loves of two women, bound together in friendship.

What is expressed in the underlined phrases is the critic's appreciation of the novel.

3. RÉSUMER

1. Contract a paragraph (p. 28-29)

1. 1. Hanif Kureishi,
The Buddha of Suburbia (p. 28)
Title : Education in the suburbs
Key sentences : in the suburbs education wasn't considered a particular advantage (l. 4).
Getting into business young was considered more important (l. 6).
Summary
Suburban kids are more concerned with earning a living at an early age than with studying. The narrator himself interrupted his college studies. As he gets better acquainted with his new friends he becomes keenly aware that in the long term culture is an essential ingredient of success.

2. Nancy Cato,
The Heart of a Continent (p. 29)
Set against the unforgiving landscape of the outback, *The Heart of a Continent* tells the story of two generations of women and a dream that came true in the Australian skies.
Alix Macfarlane's dream of building a clinic for the Aborigenes is ruined by the death of her husband in the First World War. But this dream will become reality a generation later…

2. After Heysel… (p. 30-31)

1. *Key sentences*
§1. Soccer has simply outgrown the limits of a normal sport. It has

become the setting of a tribal warfare on a vast scale.
§2. Everyone deplores the atrocities when they occur, yet no one wants to take the measures necessary to prevent them.
§3. Soccer has become a megabusiness.
§4. As the sport has been commercialized, the fans have become bestial.
§5. So long as soccer remains both big business and the stage for primitive tribal warfare, the chances are the killing will go on.

3. *Title*
Soccer violence : a pessimistic view/Business spoils soccer

4. COMPRENDRE UN TEXTE LONG

It is announced from Buckingham Palace... (p. 34-35)

Circumstances : the separation of Prince Charles and Lady Diana (December 1992).

Nature of the document : John Major's announcement of the separation of the Prince and Princess of Wales to the House of Commons.

Register of speech : formal. "Their Royal Highnesses" – words of latin origin – length of the sentences.

Lexical clue : "The House" = the House of Commons, "this House and the country."

My Life and Times (p. 35-36)

1. Title 2, *Books and Films,* suits this text best. As a matter of fact, Henry Miller does not take sides either for literature or the cinema. He clearly states in the first sentence that both appeal immensely to him. Throughout the text, he sheds light on the differences in impact on him of those two forms of art.

2. Whereas films leave a visual and **therefore** transient impact in H. Miller's memory, books provide food for his imagination. **Yet** he remembers sequences from films, **but** these do not haunt him for a long time **because** films do not set his imagination going. Color, movement and action catch his attention. **That's why** he can even sit through a poor film. He identifies easily with the people on the screen who are so real, **whereas** the image of book characters always remains vague. This is the very reason **why** books leave him totally free to imagine. **Because** words are less precise and more complex than pictures, books appeal to his mind's eye, **and (whereas)** films appeal to his real eyes.

The Book People (p. 36-37)

1. it (l. 10) = the fact that all these people "are" the great writers of the past.
it (l. 14) = knowledge.

it (l. 26) = waiting for the war to begin and end.
they (l. 29) = people (the survivors).

2. In the excerpt from *Fahrenheit 451*, Montag meets people who have learnt the works of **the greatest writers and philosophers** by heart. At first, he is **incredulous** but Granger explains that they have found **memory** the safest technique since they had to **travel** so much. Their aim is to preserve **knowledge** and they do not seek to **anger** anyone. They are waiting for the **war** to begin and end quickly. Granger expresses his **belief** that some day, even if they have to **wait** to pass the knowledge on to their children, they will be **useful**. He says it might last only until another **Dark Age** but he is confident that **Man** in the end will prevail against the forces that could rob him of his humanity.

The Lonesome Death of Poor Hattie Carroll (p. 40-42)

1. Bob Dylan's order is 4.2.1.3 but 1.4.2.3 could be possible too.

5. TRADUCTION

Ces "corrigés" ne sont que des **propositions de traduction.** Libre à vous de les améliorer.

Inférer le sens (p. 47-49)
1. *Fatty Foods Find Favor Again* (p. 47-48)
they guzzle : ils engloutissent / "se bâffrent"
a dollop : un morceau *ou simplement* de (*partitif*)
crawled down : glisse (*remarquez l'emploi du présent de narration*)
she scooped it : la recueille / la récupère (*ici*)
outlet : (*ici*) boutique / stand
sliding back : (*ici*) revenir peu à peu / retomber dans (de mauvaises habitudes)
craving : besoins maladifs / désirs

2. *Twinkle, twinkle, shooting stars* (p. 48-49)

Mayfly : *a fly* = une mouche. *Their life is little longer than* → brièveté de leur vie. Vie éphémère → **une éphémère.**

Bliss : apposé à *joyous*, *a glorious spreading of wings* → moment heureux → **bonheur absolu / félicité.**

Treadmill : s'oppose à *episode* → période longue et pénible → **dure routine.**

Harsh : associé à *rigours, cold* → **dur / sévère.**

Compulsory and rehearsed : opposés à *innocent and spontaneous* → **forcés et appris** ("répétés").

Corrigés

To overcome : surmonter.
Elfin : à rapprocher du français un elfe → **aérien**.
Were whisked away : *away* → éloignement. Les athlètes restent quelques secondes sur le podium (idée contenue dans *whisked* qui implique un mouvement preste, rapide → **on les expédia rapidement/elles furent prestement dirigées.**

Tenir compte du contexte (p. 49-50)
1. Set
1. lancé à ses trousses 2. monter contre 3. m'a donné à… 4. provoqué l'hilarité générale 5. cela le démarque 6. je mets 7. sertie 8. mettre le couvert 9. est situé, se déroule 10. tout est prêt, nous sommes fin prêts

2. Man
1. peut ne pas se traduire : il est sympathique 2. C'est… 3. jusqu'au dernier 4. il est de nouveau lui-même 5. Mon Dieu ! C'est fou ce que…

3. Then, since, for
1. à ce moment-là 2. d'ici là 3. puis 4. donc 5. Il y a aussi…
6. puisque 7. depuis 8. Cela fait combien de temps que tu ne l'as vue ? Quand l'as-tu vue pour la dernière fois ?
9. pour 10. comme 11. malgré tout 12. malgré 13. car

Définir le registre de langue (p. 50-52)
Les erreurs de registre sont portées en gras.

• Agatha Christie
"Bonjour, Mademoiselle Politt !"
La couturière répondit : "**Salut**[1]; Mademoiselle Hartnell."
Sa voix était extrêmement frêle et ses accents distingués.
A ses débuts, elle avait travaillé comme femme de chambre. "Je **voudrais pas**[2] vous déranger," continua-t-elle, "mais **vous sauriez pas**[2] par hasard si Mme Spenlow est à la maison ?"
"**J'en sais vraiment rien,**[2]" dit Mademoiselle Hartnell.
"C'est plutôt **embêtant**[3]**, tu vois.**
Je devais faire un essayage pour la nouvelle robe de Mme Spenlow cet après-midi. Elle avait dit à trois heures et demie."
Mademoiselle Hartnell consulta sa montre. "Il est la demie **et des poussières**"[4].
"Oui, j'ai frappé trois fois, mais **j'ai entendu**[2] personne bouger alors **j'me**[5] suis demandé si Madame Spenlow **était pas**[2] sortie, si elle **avait pas**[2] oublié. D'habitude, elle **oublie pas**[2] ses rendez-vous et **en plus**[6] elle veut porter sa nouvelle robe après-demain."

1. Lexique : *Bonjour*.
2. Notez l'absence de négation, incorrection grammaticale fréquente dans un registre parlé familier/vulgaire. Notez aussi l'absence d'inversion dans la question.

3. Lexique : *ennuyeux*. Notez le tutoiement abusif.
4. Lexique : *il est la demie passée*.
5. Notez la contraction en contradiction avec les "accents distingués" du locuteur.
6. Lexique : *de plus*.

- J. D. Salinger

Si vous voulez réellement **connaître mon histoire**, la première chose que vous **désirerez** savoir est le lieu où je **naquis, quelle fut** ma **triste enfance**, quelles étaient **les occupations** de mes parents avant qu'ils ne **me portent au monde**, tout ce que l'on peut lire dans un roman de Dickens, **en quelque sorte** ; je n'ai pas envie d'**évoquer** tout cela. Tout d'abord, **cela m'ennuie**, d'autre part, mes parents auraient très certainement une attaque si je racontais **quoi que ce soit** de personnel les concernant. Ils sont **fort** susceptibles **à cet égard**, en particulier mon père. Ils sont **absolument charmants, à n'en point douter**, mais ils sont aussi **extrêmement** susceptibles. D'autre part, **il n'est pas dans mes intentions de vous narrer** toute ma **pauvre existence par le menu**.

Tant au plan du lexique que des structures, la "traduction" proposée est totalement erronée.

Proposition

Si ça vous intéresse vraiment, vous allez d'abord vouloir savoir où je suis né, comment a été mon enfance pourrie, ce que faisaient mes parents avant que j'arrive, tous ces trucs qu'on trouve dans les romans de Dickens. Mais moi, j'ai pas envie d'en parler. D'abord, ces trucs-là m'embêtent et puis ils auraient chacun une attaque, mes parents, si je parlais de leur vie privée. Ils aiment pas ça, surtout mon père. Ils sont très sympa, c'est pas la question, mais ils sont vachement susceptibles. De toutes façons, je vais pas me lancer dans une foutue autobiographie, sûrement pas.

Transposer (p. 52)

1. ils ont ouvert la porte à coups de pieds 2. avant début octobre 3. du début à la fin 4. ils se risquèrent à sortir 5. il était évident que 6. Elle se contenta de 7. Il a été transporté d'urgence 8. Je me suis trompé de 9. Contentez-vous de

Moduler (p. 52-53)

1. une autre paire de manches 2. baigné de 3. tu me manques 4. il ne la remarqua qu'à peine 5. était judicieuse 6. depuis combien de temps attends-tu ? 7. il ne cesse de se plaindre 8. ordonné de me calmer 9. il n'avait plus aucune idée / il était à court d'idées 10. remettons cela à demain

Corrigés

Repérer les faux amis (p. 53-54)

2. Dans cet exercice, seules les phrases de thème sont corrigées.

1. He can make do with anything.
2. Health Care is a current issue in the United States.
3. I fail to see your point.
4. No dictionary will be at your disposal.
5. He had a tragic fate.
6. Can you possibly come tomorrow ?
7. This painting is exhibited at the Met.
8. A peace agreement was signed at the end of the conference.
9. This article did harm to him.
10. He has achieved his dream : to become an actor.
11. She has many relations abroad.
12. I feel very happy at the idea of seeing him again.
13. He is very nice.
14. He is very rude indeed.
15. Some American trains have more than a hundred carriages.

Traduire la modalité (p. 56-57)

1. … que je savais lire / ma mère avait sans doute découvert mon secret… / je ne voulais rien admettre

2. peut-être aurait-elle pu devenir le meilleur des mondes… Au début, peut-être notre monde était-il ainsi… (c'était peut-être ainsi au début…)

3. … les hommes pourraient découvrir des méthodes relativement économiques

il nous faut considérer que l'homme existe depuis environ un million d'années

ce qu'elle (la technique) pourra accomplir dans l'avenir

peut-être s'agit-il ici d'une potion magique que la race humaine est incapable d'assimiler / de supporter
il se pourrait que…

Certains pensent que l'on aurait fort peu à regretter d'une telle destruction, mais nous ne pouvons guère adopter un tel point de vue.

Traduire le passif (p. 57-58)

1. se tiennent / là où se trouve le siège de la plupart…

2. peuvent se transformer / on peut transformer / vous pouvez faire de vos restes…

3. On dit que…

4. On m'a appris… / Cela ne me fait rien qu'on me regarde…

5. il était très courant que les familles … abandonnent… / dont les médias chinois parlent périodiquement…

Les Menincs n'ont obtenu aucun détail / On leur a demandé de fournir…

6. Les responsables des chaînes en ont interdit la diffusion…

sera diffusé (*on peut ici calquer le passif*)

C'est la première publicité de ce genre qui s'adresse à…

dont on pense qu'il va faire l'objet d'une controverse

7. de sorte qu'il n'en reste pas la moindre trace
il devrait être à Paris
Pendant des mois, on ne le recherchera pas.

Lorsqu'on s'inquiètera de lui, il ne devra rester (subsister) aucune trace de sa présence ici (on ne devra pas trouver…).

Corrigés

COMPÉTENCE LINGUISTIQUE

1. LE GROUPE NOMINAL

Articles et quantificateurs (p. 66-67)

1. In Ø New York City Ø last week **the** College Entrance Examination Board issued **the** profile of Ø 1,000,000 American high school seniors who took its Scholastic Aptitude Tests (SAT). **The** profile revealed many noteworthy facts (the girls got Ø higher average scores, for example, yet had Ø less ambitious college plans than **the** boys). But one seemingly ominous result attracted most attention : **the** mean SAT scores had declined for **the** tenth year in **a** row.

3. Ø *Titanic row over Ø new exhibition*
The National Maritime Museum sought to defuse criticism of its new exhibition of artefacts from **the** wreck of **the** Titanic by promising to convene an international conference Ø next year to protect **the** heritage of ships lost on the high seas.
The museum revealed its plans to stage a conference at a press preview of **the** Titanic exhibition at Greenwich, south London.
Richard Ormond, **the** museum's director, said **the** conference would bring together representatives of seafaring nations, **the** United Nations, salvors and academics to frame a new international protocol to protect historically-significant shipwrecks.
Mr Ormond said a new protocol was needed to prevent treasure hunters "looting the sea for their own gain". He added that **the** wrecks could provide historians with time capsules which would be lost if their contents were sold and dispersed. **The** display of such objects has been condemned by Ø several groups of nautical archaeologists who argue that **the** Titanic was too recent a disaster to be significant.
But Millvina aged 82, who was nine weeks old when **the** ship sank and who also lost her father, said she had no qualms. "I think it's an excellent idea. It is part of our history."

Formation du nom et de l'adjectif (p. 67-68)

1. 1. thoughtless 2. lifeless 3. darkness 4. breathless 5. kindness
-ness est un suffixe qui sert à former un substantif à partir d'un adjectif.
-less sert à marquer le manque de…

2. 1. awareness - hazardous

2. fictional - deeply pessimistic - behaviour - writing

3. gigantic - driver - commitment - helpless - economic - technological - mastery

4. sexist - basic - practice - abilities
5. craze - convinced - strength.

3. 1. kind-hearted   2. well-known   3. age-old   4. well-paid   5. business-minded   6. wild-eyed   7. ever-brightening, ever-warming   8. densely-populated   9. self-possessed

2. LE GROUPE VERBAL

Infinitif et forme en -ing (p. 70)

1. *Rappel : la forme en -ing peut être gérondif ou nom verbal.*

1./ 6. Un certain nombre d'expressions exprimant un jugement de valeur comme *it's worth, it's no use, I can't help* sont suivies du gérondif.

2./ 5. Toutes les prépositions sont suivies du gérondif.

3. Les verbes indiquant un début, une continuation ou une fin sont suivis du gérondif.

4. Emploi de la forme progressive pour des verbes exprimant une position du corps.

7./ 8. Traduction d'un nom verbal = le fait de…

9. Les verbes de perception sont suivis soit de l'infinitif, soit du gérondif selon le point de vue que l'on adopte : résultat ou évocation de l'action en train de se passer.

10. Emploi de **to be** + base verbale en **-ing** à sens de futur.

Formes interrogatives (p. 71-72)

1. *Vous devez avoir employé ce qui est souligné.*

1. What colour is this car ?
2. Has he got a red or a blue car ? What colour pen would you like ?
   + nom
3. Which pen do you want ?
4. How does he work ?
5. How often do you walk your dog ?
6. How far from school do they live ?
7. What was the weather like ?
8. What time are we supposed to meet him ?
9. How often do you go to the pictures ?
10. Which one is the more expensive ?

2.1. **Where** was J.P. born ? **What / which** university did he go to ? 2. **How many** Valentines will be exchanged on February the 14th ? 3. **How long** has unemployment been rising steadily in G.B. ? 4. **Since when** has the theatre held performances every summer ? / Since the first performance in 1932, **how often** has the theatre held performances ? 5. **How** does much of their leisure time seem to be spent ? 6. Is the pre-eminence of London as a financial centre challenged ? 7. **How far** from where you live are Wimbledon, Barnes and Kew Gardens ? 8. **Why** didn't Earth-based observations tell you much about Venus ? 9. **Which** is more

Corrigés

popular : orange or grapefruit juice ? **What** state / **which** state supplied most of the orange juice consumed in the U.S. ? **What** country fills the gap ? 10. **How much** did / does Giotto cost ?

Modaux (p. 72-74)

	a	b	c
1. "Tired all the time ? You **can** beat it !"			X
"According to the RAC, after you have phoned for help you **should** return to your car, lock all doors except the front passenger door and wait on the embankment until help arrives."		X	
"By law, a child **must** be suitably restrained in a car in a seat belt, with a booster seat if necessary, a child car seat or a carrier."		X	
Earlier this year, the family arrived home one day to find water creeping up the garden towards the house. "We **couldn't** believe it," says Julia, "the river is normally several feet below the garden, but in the end it rose up into the house and the rooms downstairs were under a foot of water. The firemen **had to** carry the boys out through the windows. It was awful."		B→(had to): X	C→(couldn't): X
"**I cannot** have slept long for when I woke the fire was still burning brightly."	X		
He descended the stairs, almost running ; it was not far now ; now he **could** smell and feel it : the breathing and simple dark, and now he **could** manner himself to pause and wait, turning at the door, watching Miss Worsham as she followed him to the door ... Now he **could** hear the third voice, which **would** be that of Hamp's wife... William Faulkner, *Go Down, Moses.*	X (would)		X X X (coulds)
"He **must** be a Southerner, judging by those trousers," suggested Harry mischievously. " Why, Harry !" Her surprised look **must** have irritated him. F. Scott Fitzgerald, *The Ice Palace.*	X X		

	a	b	c
"Many's the night I used to sit here in this room and knit clothes for him when he was young. I even knitted trousers for him. And for all I know he **may** marry an English girl and where will I be ? He **might** go and work in England. He was staying in a house there at Christmas. He met a girl at a dance and he found out later that her father was a mayor. I'm sure she smokes and drinks. And he **might** not give me anything after all I've done for him." Iain Crichton Smith, *The Telegram.*	X X X		
"You **may** have seen my mother waltzing on ice skates in Rockefeller Center. She is seventy-eight years old now but very wiry, and she wears a red velvet costume with a short skirt… I don't know why I **should** find the fact that she waltzes so disconcerting, but I do. I avoid that neighbourhood whenever I **can** during the winter months, and I never lunch in the restaurants on the rink." John Cheever, *The Angel of the Bridge.*	X	X	X
Nuclear waste **will** not disappear. **Should** governments try to hide it away, or keep it where they **can** see it all the time ? The world's nuclear industry **may** or **may** not last. The waste it has already produced in its first half-century **will**, however be around for a very long time. Radioactive material produced today **will** still be dangerous in several million years, emitting particles that **can** cause living cells to mutate or die… *The Economist,* December 3. 1994.	X X X X X	X	X X

Corrigés

Passif (p. 75-77)

1. 1. They were immediately impressed by the power of the officials.
2. Unless Europe is united, the world will ignore its voice.
3. The Queen and Duke of Edinburgh were welcomed by delighted crowds.
4. Next month I shall suggest how this might be achieved.
5. I only read detective fiction when the characters and the background interest me.
6. This problem is going to be solved by human intelligence and ingenuity.
7. They are not to be trusted.
8. He was being shown the new offices.
9. Was she actually given the new job ?
10. Glyndebourne is mounting the production.

3. happened / beat / could not be explained / marked / was invented / defeated / played / were given / made up / came.

4. could hardly be called - were beaten - were abandoned… and left - were boarded - being sent - were taken - were raised… and treated.

Could hardly be called : the main point of interest is not the identity of who could call these people parents but the fact that **they** do not deserve the name. We may notice that this is all the more true since the agent is not mentioned.

The other passive forms have all got the same subject *they* i.e. the children. They are the focal point of interest in this short passage and therefore are the subjects of most of the verbs. Besides, one might say that the use of the passive has a cumulative effect : they are repeatedly shown as victims.

Temps (p. 77-80)

1. *Rappel*
Le prétérit est le temps de la narration au passé ; le prétérit modal indique que l'action n'est pas perçue comme réelle au moment où l'on parle. Dans les deux cas, il implique une rupture.
Le present perfect est le temps du bilan.
Le plus-que-parfait marque souvent une antériorité par rapport à une action passée.

2. 1. You**'ll recognize** me, I**'ll be wearing** a red coat.
(futur avec *will* : prévoir les faits à venir)
2. **I'm getting up** at six tomorrow.
(*be* + base verbale + *-ing* : intention de faire quelque chose dans un futur proche)
3. What **shall we do** with him…
(*shall, are we to do, are we supposed to do* : demande d'avis ou de conseils)
4. **Will you bring me** my cigarettes, please ?
(*will* : demande polie)

5. The sky is getting darker and darker, I think **it's going to** rain.
(*going to* : intention ou ici prédiction)

6. **Shall we have** dinner now ?
(*Shall* : demande d'avis)

3. was / did not care / wanted / weren't / like / are / pulled / ordered / bought / settled / had just sorted out / were starting / rang.

6. Penelope Lively,
Cleopatra's Sister (p. 79-80)

When Lucy was twenty-nine her mother **got married**. Technically, she **was remarrying**, having completed some years before the laborious process of divorcing an absent husband, but it **felt** to Lucy like a first marriage. When Maureen **told** her about Bruce – her manner a shifty combination of exultation and embarrassment – Lucy **was amazed**. As soon as she **met** him she **saw** at once that the long years of coping with Maureen's affairs **were** over. Bruce **was** manager of the branch of Tesco's at which Maureen herself **had risen** – rather surprisingly – to supervisor. He **had been betrayed** in some unspecified way by a wife who **had left** with an eight-year-old son and an immaculately equipped house in Cheam. Lucy **perceived** that he **was** entirely reliable and luxuriously in love with her mother.

"Time" and "tense" (p. 80-81)

2. a. Temps de la narration : *I remember* (**T.0** sur l'axe des temps).

as though it were... = action **simultanée à T.0** : *were* est un prétérit **modal** = irréel **du présent**.

as we came = véritable prétérit : action antérieure à *I remember*.

had just gone down = past perfect : action antérieure à *we came*.

there was = véritable prétérit : action antérieure à *I remember*, concomitante à *we came to the end*.

stopped and looked = actions succédant de peu *we came*, antérieures à *I remember*.

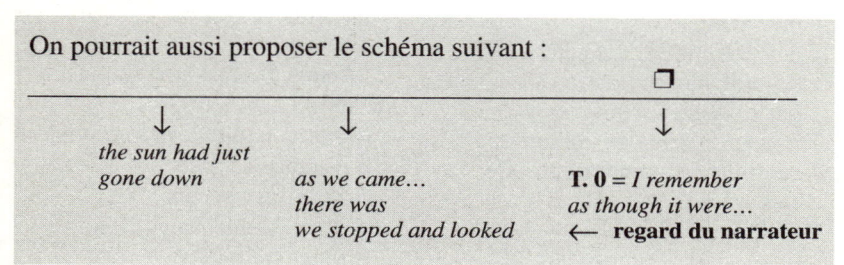

On pourrait aussi proposer le schéma suivant :

		◘
↓	↓	↓
the sun had just gone down	as we came... there was we stopped and looked	**T. 0** = *I remember* *as though it were...* ← **regard du narrateur**

Corrigés

b. Temps de la narration : *leaned back / closed her eyes* (**T. 0**)

had washed out = évocation d'une action antérieure à *leaned back and closed her eyes* (past perfect de temps).

She felt very tired : concomitant à *leaned back / closed her eyes*. A partir de cet instant, discours intérieur sans ouverture de guillemets (parfois appelé free indirect speech). Les temps des verbes dépendent par conséquent de *she realized that / could feel that...* omis dans le récit et décrivent donc une suite de faits concomitants ou même légèrement postérieurs à *she felt very tired*.

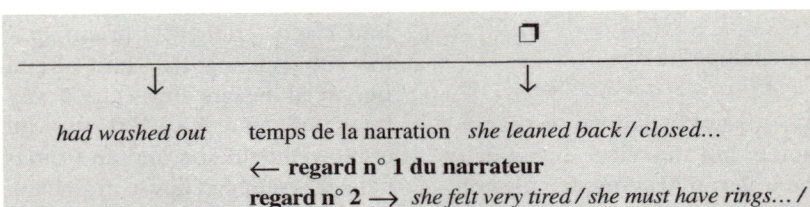

	❐	
↓	↓	↓
had washed out	temps de la narration	she leaned back / closed...
	← regard n° 1 du narrateur	
	regard n° 2 →	she felt very tired / she must have rings... / the taxi had stopped / there was...

3. *say* → a present fact
read → a past action
is recorded → a present fact
cherish, see, is → present facts or actions
are trying → focus on a present action

4.
1. Chaque énoncé comporte une forme verbale au **présent progressif**.
   a. Référence à une action qui se déroule au moment où l'on parle. Arrêt sur image.
   b. Expression de l'intention future (liée avec l'emploi de *tomorrow*)
   c. Action habituelle avec nuance de désapprobation.

2. Chaque énoncé décrit **une action/un état habituel(le)**.
   a. Action habituelle encore vraie.
   b. Etat conforme à la réalité au moment où l'on se situe dans le temps.
   c. Action habituelle passée.
   d. Action habituelle présente désapprouvée.
   e. Etat qui deviendra peut-être habituel.

3. Chaque énoncé se réfère à l'**avenir**.
   a. Futur + intention + prévision.
   b. Intention.
   c. d. Futur proche.
   e. Programme - affirmation portant sur un fait.

4. Chaque énoncé comporte un **irréel**.
   a. Irréel du passé.
   b. Irréel du présent.
   c. Irréel du présent. Léger accent sur l'idée de retard par rapport à *It's time for you to tell her.*

5. Chaque énoncé exprime un **degré de probabilité**.
   a. Simple probabilité.
   b. Grande probabilité.
   c. Certitude présente.
   d. Certitude portant sur un fait passé.
   e. Possibilité.
   f. Certitude.

Discours direct/discours indirect (p. 82)

1. *Policeman* : Er… excuse me…
Woman : Good morning, Officer. Nice day, isn't it ?
P : Funny place to…
W : Well, you see I'm writing a poem. I find churchyards so inspiring…
P : I see…
W : Would you care for a sandwich ? I've got some in this bag, help yourself !
P : That's very kind of you, thank you, but I've had my lunch already. You come here often ?
W : Yes I do, it's nice and peaceful. I can be sure not to be disturbed !
P : These graves must be very old, you can't even read the names on them.
W : That's why no one ever comes here any more.

P : Well, I must get going. Goodbye, and good luck. It was nice talking to you.

3. LA PHRASE

Place de l'adverbe (p. 84)

1. Until now, special effects in Indian cinema have **mostly** been amateurish.
However, lately, film makers have been turning to high-tech computers to give their films a fantastic feel.

Most experienced travellers **usually** keep seat belts **loosely** fastened during flight for extra comfort in case of unexpected turbulence. We would **also** like to remind you to keep your hand-baggage secure under your seat or **safely** stored in the overhead lockers.

"I **never seriously** considered the possibility that I would not emerge from prison one day. I **never** thought that a life sentence **truly** meant life and that I would die behind bars… I **always** knew that some day I would **once again** feel the grass under my feet and walk in the sunshine a free man."
Nelson Mandela.

Prépositions et particules (p. 85-86)

Ethical investments

Getting a good return **for** your savings is a high priority if you invest money, but what if you're

Corrigés

profiting **from** activities you don't approve **of** ? **Through** your pension, or personal equity plan, you could be investing **in** a company that carries **out** laboratory tests **on** animals, sells arms **to** countries **with** a poor human rights record or a company whose waste pollutes our country's rivers.
According **to** a Mintel survey, one **in** three **of** us would invest ethically even if it meant a lower return. Although a growing number of investment funds now take ethical considerations **into** account when investing your money, not all are as pure as they claim. A recent report **in** *Which* ? showed that **out of** 17 ethical funds none were ethical in every respect.

The rebirth of Glyndebourne
Glyndebourne is a legend **in** the world **of** opera - but sadly **for** scores of opera lovers, it has never been more than that. The little opera house has been packed season **after** season and, **after** friends and sponsors had exercised their priority booking, the general public was lucky to get a look **in**. Good news, then, that the new and much larger theatre opens this year - and **at** prices well **below** the average.

Multiples points de grammaire (p. 86-87)
1. 1. It had been such fun to arrange their living-room !

2. It was so lucky they should understand each other so well !
3. What a beautiful baby ! How beautiful your baby is !
4. You've grown so much !
5. Isn't it nice ?
6. What a good and nonstop reader she was !

2. *Il existe bien évidemment de nombreuses possibilités pour compléter ces phrases. Les contraintes grammaticales seules sont indiquées dans cette correction.*

1. phrase au futur ou employer *can* / modal
2. emploi du gérondif si l'on a choisi un verbe
3. commencer par un mot interrogatif (*how* par exemple) suivi d'un infinitif complet ou d'une proposition affirmative
4. employer le prétérit
5. *you would have* + participe passé
6. infinitif / *how* + infinitif complet / *that…*
7. gérondif
8. prétérit modal (par ex. *It's high time we went*)
9. présent simple ou present perfect
10. prétérit progressif (ou simple)

5. 1. She thought that it didn't make any difference.
2. It's the most exciting film I've ever seen.
3. "When I feel better, then, I'll move."
She said that when she felt better she would move.

4. We looked at each other.
5. "Would you mind giving me a drink ?"
6. He advised her to turn it off.
7. I haven't seen him for three years.
8. I didn't go, neither did she.
9. He insisted on my selling the house.

8. Michèle Roberts,
Daughters of the House (p. 89)

1. The bus-stop, **just as in the old days**, was the area of pavement outside the *Mairie*. This florid building was **now** painted salmon pink, **no longer** the faded grey that Thérèse **remembered**. She shrugged, watching the bus depart, backside of blue gas farting exhaust. She stooped to pick up her bags. [...]
She crossed the road, to take the turning that led off between the chemist's and the blacksmith's. Oh. There was **no longer** a blacksmith's. And the chemist's window, which **used to** contain antique apothecary pots in *vieux Rouen* porcelain, was **now** full of strip-lit placards of naked women scrubbing their thighs with green mittens. [...] Thérèse walked on.
She told herself that she was calm. That she was on the right road. That her feet **did recognize** its bends and loops. There was a pavement **now**, streetlamps and bus-shelters on this stretch, signs warning of sharp corners, an old people's home. **The old school had been knocked down and a new one, prefab style, built in its place** next to an asphalt playground. Only half a kilometer on did the countryside **as she remembered it** burst upon her.

Corrigés

EXPRESSION

1. MÉTHODE

Traiter un sujet de réflexion (p. 94-95)

Analyser l'énoncé d'un sujet
1/a - 2/e - 3/d - 4/c - 5/a - 6/d - 7/b - 8/e - 9/d - 10/b

2. FONCTIONS DE COMMUNICATION

Degrés de probabilité (p. 103-104)

1. "The traditional cultures are, *in any case,* doomed."	**certain**
2. If we are lucky we *may* eventually arrive at a totally integrated world culture.	**possible**
3. The noise problem that *probably* leads to a more widespread irritation than any other is domestic or neighbour noise. When your neighbours next throw a rowdy party, it is not much use calling the police because they *may not* come unless you *can* convince them there *is likely* to be a breach of the peace.	**probable** **possible** **possible possible**
4. In 2020 both books and publications *will* become much cheaper and therefore available in far greater variety. I see *no reason why* we should not have scores of national daily newspapers, and *of course we shall be able to* summon up the pages of the New York Times and the Sydney Morning Herald by dialing the right code.	**certain** **certain** **certain+ possible**
5. There *may well* be many dead pulsars moving through space. We *may be sure* that there are no such objects in the Solar System but sooner or later it is *possible* that we will encounter one of them.	**possible** **probable** **possible**
6. It is *possible* to foresee the loss of thousands of plant and animal species while at the same time the air we *breathe*, the water we *drink* and the soil in which we *grow* our food becomes ever more polluted.	**possible** **certain** **certain**
7. If they do not agree, they *will* just have to take the consequences, which *might* ultimately be fatal.	**certain** **possible**

8. We *will* be freed to devote ourselves to creative pursuits, able to educate our children in the arts and sciences. In this new golden age, we *will* start our real exploration of the universe.	certain certain
9. However much a commercial costs to make, it *will* almost *certainly* be less than the cost of showing it. T.V. advertising *can* cost anything from £ 300 to £ 30.000 for 30 seconds.	certain certain possible
10. It is *quite possible*, that by 2020 there will be manned bases on the Moon.	probable

3. RÉDACTION

Rédiger des paragraphes (p. 113-115)

1. • The twenty-fifth of June was a pleasant evening in an unpleasant summer. I was just strolling home enjoying it. In no hurry at all, and just wondering whether I would turn in for a drink somewhere when I saw this old man. He was standing on the pavement in Thanet Street, looking unwell.

• It was late and everyone had left the café except an old man who sat by the window. The two waiters knew the old man was a little drunk. And while he was a good client, they knew that if he became too drunk, he would leave without paying.

2. • Andrew Mann and his family had walked, and picnicked, and fished in the stream, but now it was time to go. They were waiting for the bus at the station. It was expected in ten minutes. But a wind had come up and the sky was filling with dark, menacing clouds.

• Margaret had declared that Ann needed a holiday. After all Ann had not been out of England for fifteen years and she ought to see France and Italy again. Ann answered that if Margaret wanted to go abroad, she'd go with her.

3.
Exemple
1. <u>Since</u> Miss Johnson was <u>not</u> good at cooking <u>nor</u> had the time to cook elaborate meals, <u>and since as well</u> she was unmarried, she was <u>accustomed to buying</u> frozen foods that she ate in front of her T.V.

4.
Here is ... The language ... In this, he largely succeeds.
The narrative begins ...
After ... and all the book ...
The balance of the novel deals with ...
He (+ *présent simple*) ...
The book ends with ...
The story is ...

Corrigés

Employer les mots de liaison
(p. 116-117)

1.
1. Indira (Gandhi) was loved **but** not spoilt. **Because** she was gawky and long-nosed, some of her relations called her an ugly duckling. Often left on her own, she learnt to take her own decisions. She was intense **and** had a searching, questioning mind. **But** above all she wanted to be worthy of her parents, **and** to help and protect them. She was proud that their pictures, along with pictures of Mahatma Gandhi, were found in hundreds of thousands of homes.

When Indira was twelve years old, her father became President of the Indian National Congress. At its 1929 session, the Congress had declared that it wanted nothing less than complete independence. **Though** she was still very young, Indira was one of those who took the pledge of independence which declared :

*The British Government in India has not only deprived the Indian people of their freedom **but** has based itself on the exploitation of the masses, and has ruined India economically, politically, culturally and spiritually. We believe, **therefore** that India must sever the British Connection.*

When told that she had to be eighteen to become a member of the Congress Party, Indira decided to form her own organisation. She gathered together a large number of boys and girls and launched the Vanar Sena or "Monkey Brigade". Its members helped the freedom movement by sewing Congress Party flags, cooking food for people **who** took part in demonstrations, giving first aid to workers injured in police conflicts and so on.

2. *Street art*
when / Yet / for / but / Here / so that

3. *The Signalman*
when / that / but / where / and / though / but / even though / that / before

DEVOIRS D'UNE HEURE

DEVOIR N°4 : MARGARET ATWOOD, THE EDIBLE WOMAN (P. 138)

1. Proposition de traduction

Marian parcourait lentement l'allée (**down** *non traduit volontairement : voir* **come up to the blackboard** = *venez au tableau*) au rythme de la douce musique dont les flots la berçaient (**to swell** → *idée d'un liquide qui se gonfle* ; **the swell** = *la houle* ; **ripple** = *clapotis/ondulation*). "Des haricots," se dit-elle. Elle trouva ceux dont l'étiquette portait la mention "vegétarien" et déposa / lança deux boîtes dans son caddie (métallique). La musique se transforma peu à peu (*chassé croisé* **into** = *se transforma* ; **swung** = *peu à peu*) en une valse aux accents métalliques ; elle continua son chemin, en essayant de se concentrer sur la liste. Cette musique lui déplaisait/la contrariait car elle connaissait son but : vous projeter doucement dans un état d'extase euphorique et réduire votre résistance à l'achat à un point tel que vous désirez tout acheter. A chaque fois qu'elle entrait dans un supermarché et qu'elle entendait les sons entraînants diffusés par des hauts parleurs invisibles, elle se souvenait d'un article qu'elle avait lu sur des vaches qui donnaient plus de lait lorsqu'on leur jouait de la musique douce.

2. Surlignez les termes importants.

lull you into a euphoric trance / cows who gave more milk… to them / like a somnambulist / deceptively-priced or subliminally-packaged/they couldn't miss / You had to buy something / abandon yourself / You let the thing… just respond/any package.

Regroupez les idées communes.

Consumers compared with cows. Lulled asleep by the music in supermarkets, commercials on TV, adverts in magazines… They are enticed to buy the *subliminally-packaged* goods, who by ?

Who are *they* ?

Advertisers, admen, all those who coax people into buying.

What is the result of the manipulation ?

Margaret Atwood's heroine chooses **any** package → the ways and means are shown to be completely absurd, useless, a waste of energy, of time and money → a very ironical outlook on the consumer society.

DEVOIR N°5 : Little Star, *Going back* (p. 139)

Compréhension

1. It has been very fashionable, trendy.
2. On the reservations.
3. *Indian unity and power, the strength of the land, Indian input,* because the *main thing people want is something to eat.*

Corrigés

4.

Attempt	Reasons for the failure
some drink	there are too many drunken Indians
some set up groups	they have to include non Indians / there are few "big heads" on the reservations
some get involved in different activities	they don't really care about the people

5. When he feels that first and foremost he belongs to his tribe.

Compétence linguistique

1. many **will go** (l. 2) : mere prediction
you**'re not leaving** (l. 8) : decision made by the subject
they **would** (l. 10) = will in a past context

2. They find they have to include **a white, a young VISTA** or **a public health representative (man/woman)**

3. *You miss the exciting discussions about what it means to be an Indian...*
He declared/maintained... they missed the exciting discussions about what it meant (means) to be an Indian.

Educated Indians have always had a difficult time working on their own reservations.
He remarked that educated Indians had always had...

They'll return to the city in two or three years, disillusioned.
He was quite sure they would return to the city two or three years after, disillusioned.

EXAMENS BLANCS

SUJET N°1 (P. 144)

Compréhension

1. The narrator is **young** because the text tells us she was *walking home from school* (l. 1) ; Lau Po also expects her to be *playing with dolls* (l. 10).
He also addresses her as *little sister* (l. 10) which gives evidence of her size and **female sex**. We also learn later on in the story that she's wearing a *dress* (l. 35).
She's of **Chinese** origin as shown by names such as Lau Po, the Tao society. Her mother speaks with *proper Chinese humility* (l. 21).

2. One detail that reveals the narrator is really gifted at chess is the fact that, after playing with Lau Po for the summer, she *played and defeated all [her] opponents one by one* (l. 19) in the outdoor games. She also wins her *first trophy* (l. 49) in the first tournament she ever goes to.

3. a. *It's only shameful if you fall down when nobody pushes you.*
In this context the narrator's mother means that you mustn't give up without even trying.

4. a.
|6.| The narrator joined a group of old men playing chess.
|3.| Lau Po taught her all he knew within a few months.
|4.| She played her first competitions in the park next to her home.
|1.| She attracted a lot of attention.
|8.| She talked her mother into allowing her to play in local tournaments.
|9.| Her mother gave her a lucky charm.
|2.| Her first opponent in the local tournament was a fifteen-year-old boy.
|5.| She was so deep in concentration that she forgot everything around her.
|7.| Her mother had her own views on chess playing.

b. The narrator joined some old men playing chess and persuaded Lau Po to play with her. Having learnt all he knew she started to play outside games to audiences of tourists. She then talked her mother into allowing her to play in local tournaments. The day she faced her first opponent, a fifteen-year-old boy, her mother gave her a lucky charm. She was so deep in concentration that she forgot everything around her and won her first trophy. Her mother was proud although she didn't approve entirely of the way she played.

5. The making of a chess champion
We witness the narrator's progress

Corrigés

from the first meeting with Lau Po to her first tournaments. We also learn about the role of her mother and of the *light wind* which is her inspiration.

Série L uniquement
6. The use of *would* shows that the same scenes repeated themselves every weekend, that the young girl played and regularly attracted audiences.

7. "Little sister, been a long time since I play with dolls," he said…
"Is luck."
"Is shame you fall down nobody push you…"
"Better to lose less, see if you really need."
"Lost eight piece this time. Last time was eleven. What I tell you ? Better off lose less !"
These sentences in **direct speech** are all spoken by the older generation of Chinese people (Lau Po, the narrator's mother). This device allows the author to give an authentic touch to her narrative and to show the older generation has not yet completely integrated American society, contrary to the young girl.

N.B. *"Want to play ?"* is different : it's **familiar** American.

8. The text reveals that the relationship between the mother and daughter is quite a subtle one. The daughter seems to know her mother well enough to achieve her ends : when she says the opposite of what she actually wants for example (l. 26-28), playing on her mother's national pride. The daughter doesn't always agree with her mother but because she respects and loves her, she knows when to keep quiet. At the same time the mother is very supportive of her daughter. She is proud of her achievements even if *with proper Chinese humility* she doesn't let it out. Their relation gives evidence of the gap between the generation of the parents who emigrated to the U. S. and the generation of the children who were born in the country but also of the deep links that bind them to their traditions and origins.

10. Traduction
Dès que je commençai à jouer, le garçon disparut, la couleur s'effaça de la pièce et je ne vis plus que mes pièces blanches et les siennes, noires, qui attendaient en face. Une brise légère commença à souffler à mes oreilles. Elle chuchotait des secrets que j'étais seule à pouvoir entendre.
"Souffle du sud," murmurait-elle. "Le vent ne laisse pas de traces." La voie m'apparut nettement et les pièges à éviter. La foule bruissa. "Chut !", "chut !" disaient les coins de la pièce. La brise se fit plus forte.

"Jette du sable par l'est pour l'égarer." Le cavalier s'avança vers le sacrifice. Le vent sifflait de plus en plus fort. "Souffle, souffle, souffle. Il ne voit rien. Il est aveugle maintenant. Fais-le pencher dans le vent, il sera plus facile à abattre."
"Échec," dis-je tandis que le vent grondait de rire. Et le vent ne fut plus qu'un petit souffle, ma respiration.

Compétence linguistique

Séries ES et S uniquement

1.
1. *You* should allow her to play in local chess tournaments.
What about allowing her to play… ?
2. *If I lose* I will bring shame on my family.
If I had lost I would have brought shame on my family.
3. *It's* been a long time since I played with dolls.
I haven't played with dolls for a long time.

2.
A man who watches me play in the park suggests that my mother allow me to play in local chess tournaments. My mother smiles graciously, an answer that means nothing. I desperately want to go, but I bite back my tongue. I know she will not let me play among strangers. So as we walk home I say in a small voice that I don't want to play in the local tournament. They will have American rules. If I lose I will bring shame on my family.

3.
Une petite foule de badauds, chinois et touristes, s'assemblait habituellement autour de moi en fin de semaine pour me voir jouer et battre mes adversaires un à un. Ma mère se joignait à la foule lors de ces compétitions de plein air. Elle se tenait assise fièrement sur le banc, confiant à mes admirateurs, avec une humilité toute chinoise, "Elle, chance."

TABLE DES ILLUSTRATIONS

Page 32 - Portrait de O J Simpson, © Gamma Liaison.

Page 107 - Illustration de la couverture de *The Citadel of Chaos* par Emmanuel, © Editions Puffin Books, 1983 / DR.

ACKNOWLEDGMENTS

For permission to reproduce copyright material the Editors and Publishers are indebted to the following Authors, Literary Executors and Publishers :

FARRAR, STRAUS & GIROUX, Inc. for excerpts from "Baby" and "Old Complaints Revisited" from *I, ETCETERA* by Susan Sontag. Copyright © 1974, 1978 by Susan Sontag. Reprinted by permission of Farrar, Straus & Giroux, Inc.

Rights reserved for *Films and Filming*, November 1983.

AURUM PRESS Ltd 1978 for an extract from *Masters of Comic Book Art* by P.R. Garriock.

WILLIAM MORROW & Co for an excerpt from *Harlequin* by Morris West.

FABER & FABER Ltd 1990 for an excerpt from *The Buddha of Suburbia* by Hanif Kureishi.

US News and World Report, April 25, 1988, Washington, © Governor Richard Lamm.

BLACK SPARROW PRESS for an excerpt from *Wait Until Spring Bandini* , Copyright © 1983 by John Fante and reprinted with permission of Black Sparrow Press.

Newsweek, April 24, 1989, © New York Times Syndicate.

The Independent for "Wise ruling provokes calls of double standards" by David Usborne, © *The Independent*, September 11, 1994.

The Guardian Weekly, December 20, 1992.

THE ESTATE OF HENRY MILLER for an excerpt from *My Life and Times* by Henry Miller, © The Estate of Henry Miller. All rights reserved.

DON CONGDON ASSOCIATES, Inc. for an excerpt from *Fahrenheit 451* by Ray Bradbury, © 1954 Ray Bradbury.

The Economist, November 21, 1992, © *The Economist*, London, November 21, 1992.

WITMARK & SONS, WARNER BROS MUSIC for *The Lonesome Death of Hattie Carroll* by Bob Dylan, © 1964 by Witmark & Sons pour le monde, PECF pour : France, territoires SACEM, Luxembourg, Europe n°1, Belgique et territoires SABAM.

GRANADA PUBLISHERS for an excerpt from *The Female Eunuch* by Germaine Greer.

MICHAEL JOSEPH Ltd for an excerpt of *The Sacred Clowns* by Tony Hillerman. (1993).

The Guardian Weekly for "Fatty Foods Find Favor Again", by Jay Mathews, July 25, 1993, © *The Guardian Weekly*.

The Sunday Times for "Twinkle, Twinkle, Shooting Stars" by Nick Pitt, August 2, 1992.

AITKEN AND STONE, London, for an excerpt from "Tape-Measure Murder ", in *Miss Marple's Final Cases* by Agatha Christie.

Rights reserved for an excerpt from *The Limits of Human Power* by Bertrand Russell.

The Guardian Weekly, October 2, 1994.

CHATTO & WINDUS, Random House for an excerpt from "The Empty Lunch-Tin" in *Antipodes* by David Malouf.

The Economist, January 21, 1995, © *The Economist*, London, January 21, 1995.

WILLIAM HEINEMAN Ltd 1985, for an excerpt from *Under the Banyan Tree* by R.K. Narayan, © R. K. Narayan, 1985. All rights reserved.

The Guardian Weekly for "Titanic row over new exhibition" by Edward Pikington, October 9, 1994, © *The Guardian Weekly*.

PAN BOOKS for an excerpt from *"B " is for Burglar* by Sue Grafton, 1985.

FONTANA PAPERBACKS for an excerpt from *The Seven Ages* by Eva Figes (1986).

The Economist, July 30, 1994, © *The Economist*, London, July 30, 1994.

HOUGHTON MIFFLIN Co for an excerpt from *The Ballad of the Sad Café and Collected Short Stories* by Carson McCullers. Copyright 1936, 1941, 1942, 1950, © 1955 by Carson McCullers, © renewed 1979 by Flora V. Lasky. Reprinted by permission of Houghton Mifflin Co. All rights reserved.

PENGUIN BOOKS Ltd, UK for an excerpt from *Cleopatra's Sister* by Penelope Lively (Viking, 1993), Copyright © Penelope Lively, 1993.

DON CONGDON ASSOCIATES, Inc. for an excerpt from *The Martian Chronicles* by Ray Bradbury, Copyright © 1951 Ray Bradbury.

Woman and Home Magazine, June 1994.

VIRAGO PRESS Ltd 1992 for an excerpt from *Daughters of the House* by Michèle Roberts.

The Economist, July 20, 1991, © *The Economist*, London, July 20, 1991.

The Sun for their *Stars column* by Suzie Elliott, September 20, 1982, © *The Sun*.

PUFFIN BOOKS, Penguin Books Ltd UK, for an excerpt from *The Citadel of Chaos* by Steve Jackson, Copyright © Steve Jackson, 1983. All rights reserved.

Knight-Ridder Financial, Chicago, Illinois for the article *The Catcher in the Rye* by Paul Engle, from *Chicago Sunday Tribune Magazine of Books*, July 15, 1951. Reprinted with permission of Knight-Ridder Financial. © 1995 Knight-Ridder Financial, Chicago, Illinois.

The Times, April 21, 1989 for an excerpt adapted from an article by Heather Kirby, *The Times*, London, April 21, 1989, © Times Newspapers Limited, 1989.

ALFRED A. KNOPF Inc./PETERS FRASER & DUNLOP for an excerpt from *The Middle Ground* by Margaret Drabble, © Alfred A. Knopf Inc./Peters Fraser & Dunlop.

AVON BOOKS for an excerpt from *The Arrangement* by Elia Kazan.

ANDRE DEUTSCH Ltd 1979 for an excerpt from *The Edible Woman* by Margaret Atwood, © Margaret Atwood, 1969, 1980. All rights reserved.

PENGUIN BOOKS for the excerpt by Little Star (Tribe unknown) 1970, from *Native American Testimony* by Peter Nabokov, edited by Peter Nabokov, © Peter Nabokov, 1978, 1991. All rights reserved.

HARPER COLLINS Publishers Inc. for an excerpt from Alan Sillitoe. Rights reserved.

ABNER STEIN for an excerpt from *The Joy Luck Club* by Amy Tan.

FABER AND FABER, 1989 for an excerpt from *The Remains of the Day* by Kazuo Ishiguro, © Kazuo Ishiguro, 1989. All rights reserved.

GOTHAM ART & LITERARY AGENCY Inc. for an excerpt from *A Suspension of Mercy* by Patricia Highsmith.

AVON BOOKS, The Hearst Corporation, for an excerpt from *The War Between the Tates* by Alison Lurie, Copyright © Alison Lurie (1974).

The authors tend their apologies to any owner of copyright material that they have been unable to trace and whose rights may have been unwittingly infringed.

Achevé d'imprimer en juillet 1996 dans les ateliers de Normandie Roto Impression s.a.
à Lonrai (Orne)   N° d'imprimeur : 961239   Dépôt légal : 15507 – juillet 1996